Dedication

In gratitude for many wonderful

Sunday School teachers, including

Mrs. Bailey, Dale Clayton, Larry Huff,

Dick Morris, and Phil Moore.

And in gratitude to Bill Kilday,

who made this book possible.

Kevin Slimp

Publisher, Market Square Books

Our Ten Favorite Sunday School Lessons

Ten Adult Sunday School Lessons by Clergy
of the Holston Conference

Bill Kilday

and his friends from the Holston Conference
of the United Methodist Church

Market
Square
BOOKS

Our Ten Favorite Sunday School Lessons

Ten Adult Sunday School Lessons by Clergy of the Holston Conference

©2024 Market Square Publishing, LLC

books@marketsquarebooks.com
141 N. Martinwood, Suite 103-2   Knoxville, Tennessee 37923

ISBN: 978-1-950899-82-1

Printed and Bound in the United States of America
Cover Illustration & Book Design ©2024 Market Square Publishing, LLC

Compiled by Bill Kilday
Editor: Sheri Carder Hood
Post-Process Editor: Ken Rochelle
Design: Kevin Slimp

Scripture quotations used with permission from:

CEB

Scripture quotations from the COMMON ENGLISH BIBLE. © Copyright 2011 COMMON
ENGLISH BIBLE. All rights reserved. Used by permission. (www.CommonEnglishBible.com).

NRSVUE

Scripture quotations taken from the New Revised Standard Version Updated Edition.
Copyright © 2021 National Council of Churches of Christ in the United States of America.
Used by permission. All rights reserved worldwide.

NIV

Scriptures marked NIV are taken from the NEW INTERNATIONAL VERSION (NIV):
Scripture taken from THE HOLY BIBLE, NEW INTERNATIONAL VERSION ®. Copyright©
1973, 1978, 1984, 2011 by Biblica, Inc.™. Used by permission of Zondervan.

MES

THE MESSAGE: THE BIBLE IN CONTEMPORARY ENGLISH (MES):
Scripture taken from THE MESSAGE: THE BIBLE IN CONTEMPORARY ENGLISH,
copyright©1993, 1994, 1995, 1996, 2000, 2001, 2002. Used by
permission of NavPress Publishing Group

Contents

Lesson 1

Psalm 51 – A Prayer for Healing and Renewal

Lesson by Andy Ferguson

About the lesson writer:

After forty-one years in the local church, Rev. Andy Ferguson is now retired after serving churches of all sizes in Holston Annual Conference. He still loves Sunday School—where you will find him most Sundays.

Scripture Lesson
Psalm 51:1-17

Have mercy on me, O God, according to your steadfast love; according to your abundant mercy, blot out my transgressions.

Wash me thoroughly from my iniquity, and cleanse me from my sin.

For I know my transgressions, and my sin is ever before me.

Against you, you alone, have I sinned, and done what is evil in your sight, so that you are justified in your sentence and blameless when you pass judgment.

Indeed, I was born guilty, a sinner when my mother conceived me.

You desire truth in the inward being; therefore teach me wisdom in my secret heart.

Purge me with hyssop, and I shall be clean; wash me, and I shall be whiter than snow.

Let me hear joy and gladness; let the bones that you have crushed rejoice.

Hide your face from my sins, and blot out all my iniquities.

Create in me a clean heart, O God, and put a new and right spirit within me.

Do not cast me away from your presence, and do not take your holy spirit from me.

Restore to me the joy of your salvation, and sustain in me a willing spirit.

Then I will teach transgressors your ways, and sinners will return to you.

Deliver me from bloodshed, O God, O God of my salvation, and my tongue will sing aloud of your deliverance.

O Lord, open my lips, and my mouth will declare your praise.

For you have no delight in sacrifice; if I were to give a burnt offering, you would not be pleased.

The sacrifice acceptable to God is a broken spirit; a broken and contrite heart, O God, you will not despise.

Psalm 51:1-17 (NRSVUE)

The Occasion for our Focus on Psalm 51

Ash Wednesday marks the beginning of Lent. On that day, we traditionally offer a service of Marking with Ashes. Often, we turn to Psalm 51 to give words to that holy day. We can study Psalm 51 to prepare for Ash Wednesday, or we can explore the work of confession and repentance any time.

It's Us

The truth is that none of us are good at confession. And that is a problem because today's prayer is Psalm 51, and it is all about confession. Psalm 51 stands as God's case that confession is good for the soul, although we are certain that cannot possibly be the case.

No one likes to be criticized; no one likes it when the criticism is on target and, therefore, cannot be denied. But, worse than criticism from others is the self-criticism of confession. There is no wiggle room when we are the ones pointing out our own failures.

In the public sphere, we can think of two ways to deal with confession:

- We might enter a guilty plea in court, a legal confession. It means we will do time in the slammer—or maybe not. By entering a confession in court, what happens next is in the hands of judges and attorneys, who probably are not our friends. It sounds grim.

- We might fight the charges, whether in court or the public arena (think public figures at every level). The best defense is a good offense. Even if they decide you did whatever you're charged with, people will still respect your willingness to fight. Fighting the charges usually requires money, position, or both. It also requires thick skin. For those of us who hate the idea of confession, this is an attractive option. Even if convicted, we never have to do it to ourselves.

If you are wondering how a sweet psalm from the Bible has stirred up so much angst in a Sunday School class down at the church, just remember this: the Bible can get in our faces pretty fast. We usually keep the pages closed until Sunday mornings. Even then, we read it in a stained-glass voice that makes it seem like something far from everyday living. We have learned to handle our failures and losses in business-like ways; thus, we have pushed aside the idea of standing before God to confess anything. But what if all these half-measures fail to provide the peace we need? Pull out Psalm 51; it will give us the words.

The best way to read Psalm 51 is to imagine standing before God, hat in hand, determined to make everything right with God. Let's get started.

Making a List

We should start making a list of our everyday losses, failures, and mistakes that might call for confession. We are already squirming in our chairs at the idea of creating such a list. This list is just a start; you can make your own. "Been there, done that, got the T-shirt to prove it," as the saying goes. Below are a few examples.

While making a left turn in town, a fender-bender is better left to cooler heads than ours. We leave it either to the investigating officer or insurance adjusters. This is why we are carefully taught not to admit guilt while examining the damage. We might hurt our case if we say too much. Even after the damage has been repaired, we never say to the other driver, "I'm sorry."

Author Robin DiAngelo explains that when white people are confronted by our subtle or not-so-subtle racism, we are quick to take offense at the charge and defend ourselves. This quickness to take offense at the suggestion that we are part of racism has a name: "white fragility." Thus, white folks (like this author) will not even be curious about or explore our racism because we quickly react with indignation; we are offended. Examination and confession in this area are quickly derailed.[1]

Of course, we all have relationships. Things go wrong. Misunderstandings happen. Sometimes, we are slimeballs. Relationships offer plenty of opportunities to practice confession. As the great philosopher Roger Miller sang in his song: "It's my belief pride is the chief cause in the decline of the number of husbands and wives."[2]

We have all had the experience of 'fessing up to something like a cafeteria food fight in Mrs. Dunagan's sixth-grade class. It was so magnificent it had a name: The Great Tangerine Peel Deal. We were all involved— only some of the instigators got off because they did not confess. Of course, because they did not tell their part, the teacher never considered that they could be involved. (As you can tell, I hold no lingering resentment for this long-ago event.)

Psalm 51, our prayer for today, is about confessing our sins and shortcomings—and knowing it will be good for us. Ash Wednesday is coming, and this prayer is the center of special services on that day. I'm telling you this so you can get your shirt cleaned and pressed or plan to be somewhere else.

---

[1]   Robin DiAngelo, White Fragility, *Why It's So Hard for White People to Talk about Racism* (Beacon Press, 2018).

[2]   Roger Miller, "Husbands and Wives," Words and Music (Smash Records, 1966) Vinyl.

What Does Confession Accomplish?

Have you ever wondered why God is such an easy touch when forgiving sin?

King David committed adultery and misused his authority with Bathsheba. David then had her husband killed to cover up his adultery. He did some pretty bad stuff. Later, it was said of King David that he was a man after God's own heart. What a turnaround! What did David do to deserve that?

Further, have you noticed how prayers of confession in church—even pretty harsh prayers—are immediately followed by words of assurance and pardon?[3] It's quick, and then we move on.

On January 13, 2021, Brené Brown did a podcast segment entitled "Words, Actions, Dehumanization, and Accountability" in which she explained that we are quick to pour on shame when we see something going wrong. We are quick to treat wrongdoers of all kinds as less than truly human. Thus, punishment and violence against them become easy. "Lock 'em up" is the joyous shout. But, she said, our dehumanizing and shaming do not encourage people to change for the better. And the God of the Bible has seemed to understand this from the beginning of time. "Helping people to change their evil ways and their destructive attitudes," she said, "begins

---

[3] "Prayers of Confession and Words of Assurance," *The United Methodist Hymnal* (The United Methodist Publishing House, 1989), 890-892.

with believing in another's ability to grow and change."[4]

As Frances Shuster says on the website of Results Coaching Global, "True accountability aligns with the essential mindset of a coach—believing in another's ability to grow and excel. When we truly hold this belief, we hold others as "able" while they hold themselves accountable."[5]

Thus, there is little reason to offer prayers of confession to a god (little "g") who does not love or delight in us. The God of the Bible is the God of "steadfast love" and "abundant mercy," who is able and ready to wash us from every sin. When our God is this sort of God, then confession is not just an admission of failure; it is also a statement of possibility.

Being the Prophet Nathan, confronting sinners like King David would be righteously satisfying. But remember, there is a limit to our calling out or shaming a guilty party. Throwing shame on another person is NOT the point of this psalm. Instead, Psalm 51 offers the belief that we can return and restore our most important relationships. Change is possible.

If we condemn someone to death (like the woman caught in adultery), we end all chance that the guilty one may have a change of heart. This is not to say

---

[4] Brené Brown, "Words, Actions, Dehumanization, and Accountability," *Unlocking Us,* January 13, 2021. Podcast, https://brenebrown.com/podcast/brene-on-words-actions-dehumanization-and-accountability/.

[5] Frances Shuster, website of *Results Coaching Global,* https://resultscoachingglobal.com/accountability-the-two-sided-coin-of-blame-and-ownership/.

that the guilty should walk away without facing the consequences of their actions. As Brené Brown points out, people should be held accountable—not shamed or dehumanized.[6] Accountability expects change; shaming and dehumanization just tear down.

Psalm 51 is a prayer to God for help and deliverance from all that is tearing us down. This prayer of confession works because our God is that sort of God.

Read Psalm 51 Responsively

This Psalm may be read by a leader and all other voices OR by two voices (Reader 1 and Reader 2). When the class is being held online, two voices will work better. Begin the responsive reading of the Psalm with verse 1.

In the Bible, the Psalm is introduced by a note that we call a "superscription." It is part of the biblical text but not part of the prayer.

"To the leader: A Psalm of David, when the Prophet Nathan came to him, after he had gone in to Bathsheba."

Leader:
Have mercy on me, O God,
according to your steadfast love;
according to your abundant mercy
blot out my transgressions.

---

6 Brené Brown, "Words, Actions, Dehumanization, and Accountability," *Unlocking Us*, January 13, 2021. Podcast, https://brenebrown.com/podcast/brene-on-words-actions-dehumanization-and-accountability/.

All:

Wash me thoroughly from my iniquity,

and cleanse me from my sin,

For I know my transgressions,

and my sin is ever before me.

Leader:

Against you, you alone, have I sinned,

and done what is evil in your sight,

so that you are justified in your sentence

and blameless when you pass judgment.

All:

Indeed, I was born guilty,

a sinner from the moment my mother conceived me.

Leader:

You desire truth in the inward being;

therefore teach me wisdom in my secret heart.

Purge me with hyssop, and I shall be clean;

wash me, and I shall be whiter than snow.

All:

Let me hear joy and gladness;

let the bones that you have crushed rejoice.

Hide your face from my sins,

and blot out all of my iniquities.

Leader:

Create in me a clean heart, O God,

and put a new and right spirit within me.

Do not cast me away from your presence, and do not take
your holy spirit from me.

All:

Restore to me the joy of your salvation,

and sustain in me a willing spirit.

Then I will teach transgressors your ways,

and sinners will return to you.

Leader:

Deliver me from bloodshed, O God,

O God of my salvation,

and my tongue will sing aloud of your deliverance.

All:

O Lord, open my lips,

and my mouth will declare your praise.

Leader:

For you have no delight in sacrifice;

if I were to give a burnt offering, you would not be pleased.

The sacrifice acceptable to God is a broken spirit; a broken

and contrite heart, O God, you will not despise.[7]

Leader:

Let all God's people say together ...

All:

AMEN.

---

[7]   *New Revised Standard Version, Psalm 51* (Division of Christian Education of the National Council of the Churches of Christ in the USA, 1989).

Points for Reflection

The Bad News

Psalm 51 calls our attention to a persistent failure of the human situation: sin. In short, Psalm 51 is not just about Israel or David or some unknown ancient psalmist. It is also about us! It is about who we are and how we are as individuals, families, and churches. Sin permeates our lives. It is embarrassing. This is the bad news.

Reflect: List one or more occasions when you were in the wrong. Consider journaling or sharing with trusted friends.

The Good News

Psalm 51 is also about God's nature. The good news is that God can forgive sinners and can re-create people. Israel's life is an example. David's life is an example. The psalmist's life is an example, too. By the grace of God, a persistently disobedient people become partners with God in an everlasting covenant. By the grace of God, dull and disobedient disciples of Jesus (both the original Twelve and all of us today) become those who can turn the world upside-down. This is good news.

Reflect: Does it help to know that God expects to welcome and heal us from sin?

Ours is a religion that sets a high moral standard and, at the same time, offers mercy to those who have been hurt and those who have inflicted hurt. In Christ, we experience both. Thus, the psalm is a model; it teaches us the words to say and the attitude to bring when we are ready to turn away from our hurtful ways and return to God's ways.

What happens when we pray this psalm?

How does repentance work in us?

We have lived too long to sit comfortably with a quick prescription of this psalm to someone feeling guilty. In the course of life, we hurt one another. Sometimes in small ways, sometimes in grievous ways. Too often, we have seen someone sidestep their responsibility by declaring, "I have made it right with God. And, if God has forgiven me, then you must forgive me, too." Responsibility avoided. That is not the intention of this psalm.

Instead, Psalm 51 declares the deep connection between our human moral failures and our standing before God. As Maude used to tell her husband each night on TV, "God will get you for that."[8] There is a connection here. To sin in our most important relationships is to sin against God. To restore our most important relationships is to restore ourselves to God. They are necessarily connected.

"Me Too"

The connection of Psalm 51 with David's sin against Bathsheba and his murder of her husband, Uriah, leads us to think of the "Me Too" movement in this country. In recent years, we have heard too many women we care about speak up to say, "Me Too." The pattern of male sexual abuse against women is too common.

Have you heard someone you care about say, "Me Too," sharing that they have been sexually harassed? Or bullied?

---

[8] *Maude,* an American sitcom television series originally broadcast on the CBS from September 12, 1972, until April 22, 1978.

13

Both King David and modern-day abusers play tough until they are forced into public confrontations in legal court or the court of public opinion. The invitation of this psalm to King David or anyone is to look in the mirror and admit, "Yes, I did that." It could be the beginning of accountability.

What Happens When We Pray Psalm 51?

Well, often not much. We read the psalm or attend Ash Wednesday services and go through the motions. No one expects us to be crushed with guilt according to the liturgical calendar. Still, we are creating a file with each reading and each Ash Wednesday—for the day we will need it.

Think about that superscription at the beginning of the Psalm. It tells us that David's shameful actions triggered the writing of the psalm.

If we live long enough, a day will come when our words or actions will leave us needing a prayer that we do not know how to pray. We will find ourselves feeling as low as a snake on hot asphalt getting run over by a convoy of eighteen-wheelers. And we will know that we deserve to stay right there. Then, we will reach back into our file and recall the prayer of Psalm 51. We'll remember that this prayer does not begin with the psalm writer; it begins with God, whose nature is mercy and steadfast love. When we remember that God works first, we can pray for a new beginning. Then, we can get up from the asphalt beating we so richly deserve.

What shameful actions have broken us so deeply that we need a PRAYER like this to speak to God?

Maybe we do not need this prayer today; still, the day will come. And Psalm 51 will give us the words to say when we don't have a prayer in this world.

Conclusion

Standing before God and offering a prayer of confession like Psalm 51 can be the first step toward a new beginning. Keep this prayer handy. The day might come when we—like David—will need it, too. It is a prayer that begins with God's love and mercy. God's desire to love us is the only foundation sturdy enough to build new beginnings.

Reflection Questions

Who in society, in America, or in our circle of friends might need to be praying this prayer today?

As we list those who should be praying this prayer, are we thinking about straightening somebody out so they will be ashamed of what they have done? Or are we thinking about restoring them to the good graces of our community?

Is everyone a candidate for forgiveness and restoration?

Lesson 2

Out from the Shadows

Lesson by Glenna B. Manning

About the lesson writer:

Glenna Manning is a retired ordained deacon who served churches in the Holston Conference in the role of Pastor of Discipleship. In retirement, she continues to love to teach and leads Sunday morning classes and weekday studies at Concord United Methodist in Knoxville, Tennessee. Glenna's other passions are traveling with her beloved husband and spending time with her family and cherished friends.

Scripture Lesson
Luke 15:1-3, 11-32

Now all the tax collectors and sinners were coming near to listen to him. And the Pharisees and the scribes were grumbling and saying, "This fellow welcomes sinners and eats with them." So he told them this parable:

Then Jesus said, "There was a man who had two sons. The younger of them said to his father, 'Father, give me the share of the wealth that will belong to me.' So he divided his assets between them. A few days later the younger son gathered all he had and traveled to a distant region, and there he squandered his wealth in dissolute living. When he had spent everything, a severe famine took place throughout that region, and he began to be in need. So he went and hired himself out to one of the citizens of that region, who sent him to his fields to feed the pigs. He would gladly have filled his stomach with the pods that the pigs were eating, and no one gave him anything. But when he came to his senses he said, 'How many of my father's hired hands have bread enough and to spare, but here I am dying of hunger! I will get up and go to my father, and I will say to him, "Father, I have sinned against heaven and before you; I am no longer worthy to be called your son, treat me like one of your hired hands."' So he set off and went to his father. But while he was still far off, his father saw him and was filled with compassion; he ran and put his arms around him and kissed him. Then the son said to him, "Father, I have sinned against heaven and before you; I am no longer worthy to be called your son." But the father said to his slaves, "Quickly, bring out a robe—the best one— and put it on him; put a ring on his finger and sandals on his feet. And get the fatted calf and kill it, and let us eat and celebrate, for this son of mine was dead and is alive again; he was lost and is found!" And they began to celebrate.

Now his elder son was in the field, and as he came and approached the house, he heard music and dancing. He called one of the slaves and asked what was going on. He replied, "Your brother has come, and your father has killed the fatted calf because he has got him back safe and sound." Then he became angry and refused to go in. His father came out and began to plead with him. But he answered his father, "Listen! For all these years I have been working like a slave for you, and I have never disobeyed your command, yet you have never given me even a young goat so that I might celebrate with my friends. But when this son of yours came back, who has devoured your assets with prostitutes, you killed the fatted calf for him!" Then the father said to him, "Son, you are always with me, and all that is mine is yours. But we had to celebrate and rejoice, because this brother of yours was dead and has come to life; he was lost and has been found."

Luke 15:1-3, 11-32 (NRSVUE)

Introduction

Of all the parables told by Jesus, this one, which we now commonly call the Parable of the Prodigal (or Lost) Son, is perhaps my favorite and the one I have studied the most, for in it, we come face to face with both the nature of humanity and the nature of God. Another reason this is probably my favorite is that I can readily identify with the three major figures in the story.

At times in my life, I have felt separated from God and known of that stubborn desire to do things my own way—accountable to no one. As a daughter of beloved parents and the sister to two brothers, I know all too well about sibling rivalry and the desire to be "loved best" or "the favored child." And as a mother, I recognize the heart of the father, for I too have known the heartache, anguish, and longing for children—not just my children, but all God's children—to choose the path of righteousness and to offer grace in the spirit of forgiveness when they do not.

Yes, I know the story's figures well, for I have been all three. As we move into the parable told by Jesus, perhaps you will identify yourself with all three as well.

Background

This story is the last of three parables in Luke 15 regarding lostness and the joy of being found—the other two being the story of the lost sheep and the lost coin. In this third parable, it is no longer "things" that are lost but "people." The crowd to whom Jesus is telling the parable are noted as tax collectors, sinners, Pharisees, and legal experts. It is to these people he is speaking, and as such, we interpret the story in light of this audience. Perhaps a notable characteristic of the listening audience groups is their interest in "self," which could be self-righteousness or a regard only for self (narcissism). In either account, the people to whom Jesus was speaking looked at the world only from their viewpoint, with little to no grace or regard for others.

The parable told by Jesus centers around two sons and their father. It is not the first time we hear stories of two sons. Cain and Abel, Ishmael and Isaac, Esau and Jacob, and the sons of Joseph, Manasseh and Ephraim. The listeners to this story would be familiar with these family stories and automatically think the younger son was to be the most righteous, as was true in the other biblical stories.

However, in this story, it appears to be the opposite. It is the egregious action of the younger son who brazenly asks his father for his share of the estate before his father's death that will earn him the title of "lost" or "prodigal" and sets the stage for the parable. Some scholars interpret that for the younger son to ask for "his" share of the estate was the same as wishing the father death. Others disagree but feel that the request was dishonorable to the father because it was a fleeing from family and all for which the family stood. In Jewish culture, honor was highly valued. However, at a minimum, one may view the prodigal's actions as selfish and without concern for anyone else but himself.

The "Younger" Son

Upon receiving his share of his father's estate from his obliging father, the younger son sets out and leaves his family, friends, and homeland to live as he wants to live. Scripture (Luke 15:13) tells us, depending upon translations, that he "squandered" (scattered, wasted, dissipated) his wealth in "excessive" (foolish, riotous, extravagant, wild, debaucherous, reckless) living. As the reader of the parable, we are left to fill in the blank about what the prodigal's behavior encompassed, but, needless to say, he was NOT making good decisions.

For a moment, let us put ourselves in the minds of those being told the parable and what they may have thought about this younger son:

- **Tax Collectors:** "What a waste of money! Now there is less for me to squeeze out of the father of the estate!"

- **Sinners:** "So, I've been there and done that. What's the problem? No one's perfect! So he wasted the money. There is always more where that came from! He can join the rest of us who are unredeemable!"

- **Pharisees:** "Foolish father. I could have told him from the beginning that giving the kid the money wouldn't end well and would end up in unrighteous living."

- **Legal Experts:** "According to the Jewish law, it is a sin for the son to act so recklessly and bring such dishonor to his family. His name should be erased from the family ancestry!"

Questions:

Of those from the listening office noted, with whose viewpoint would you most identify? Why?

Are there other comments to those listed you would add if you had been in the audience?

Now imagine yourself in the mind of the father who gave the money. Why would he do such a seemingly careless thing? Could it be, he thought:

- "Perhaps this will be good for him to get out and live independently and make his own way?"

- "Maybe he will get this foolishness out of his system and return home a more mature young man"?

- "Perhaps he will appreciate what he had while living on his own and seeing how hard it is to make it"?

- "Maybe it will be good for him to get out from the shadow of his older brother and discover who he really is"?

Today, as parents, or in listening to other parents, have we heard similar thoughts as these when they yield to, encourage, or help finance a child who is yearning to get away from home?

If we equate the father figure in the story with God, what is the similarity?

(Possible Answer) Like the father, God gives us abundant gifts—none of which we really deserve, yet the gifts are given anyway. And with the gifts come the choice and ability to receive them with gratitude and thanksgiving, acknowledging the giver, or the choice of squandering them away in selfish living without thought to the giver.

As the story proceeds, the younger son eventually runs out of money; in addition, there is a strong famine in the region where he now lives. Out of necessity, he takes on a job and is sent to feed the pigs. It is there he finds himself longing to be fed, even if it is the same food as the pigs. But no one takes notice of him.

One definition of living in "poverty" is living without shelter, food, clothing, and relationships with others who care about them. It is in this sense that we can now say the younger son was living in total depravity and poverty. In our culture, we often term this as "hitting rock bottom." Once the bottom is reached, there is nowhere further down to go, and the only hope lies in reversing the trend. For the younger son, it is a time of recognition of his waywardness, remembering what he left, and seeking his way back.

Question:

Now, let's pause again to wonder how we might respond to the younger son's desire to make his way back home. Which of the following might we tend to think?

- He made his bed (choice) and will just have to live with it.

- Is he truly repentant or conniving to come home thinking he will get back into the father's good grace and perhaps ask for more money?

- He can come back, but there will be a cost to pay.

- It will be good to have him home again; he is forgiven.

As the parable goes, the father welcomes the younger son home with kisses and prepares a celebration. The younger son is no longer living in the shadow of death; instead, he is clothed in a fine robe, a ring is placed on his finger, and sandals are slipped onto his feet—all of which are a sign of family belonging. After the clothing, a calf is sacrificed, and the party and the rejoicing begin.

Question:

Despite all his losses, what did the younger son still possess?

The Elder Son

All seems well back at the family estate until we finally hear from the elder son. Throughout the entire parable, the elder son seems to hide in the shadows. We do not hear his opinion about the father giving the younger son a share of the estate. We do not hear any words he has to say to his brother for making such an audacious request. For someone in such a significant role in the family as the eldest son, his silence is deafening. Yet, again, we might make inferences about his silence.

Question:

What do you think? As the youngest son left the household, do you think the elder son was:

- Delighted the younger brother was leaving as he was lazy and did nothing to help anyway?

- Resentful that the younger brother was getting away from all the responsibilities to live a carefree life? Why was he so lucky?

- Angry that the younger brother would bring such disgrace to the family name?

- Grateful he is gone because the elder son liked being in control, and now he had the whole place to himself?

Perhaps we get a hint as to the elder son's feelings when he finally speaks, and we hear his response to the father upon the return of the younger son:

> *"Look, I've served you all these years, and I never disobeyed your instruction. Yet you've never given me as much as a young goat so I could celebrate with my friends. But when this son of yours returned, after gobbling up your estate on prostitutes, you slaughtered the fattened calf for him."*
>
> **Luke 15:29-30 (CEB)**

Yes, it all pours out! Resentment, anger, rage, injustice, and superiority are just a few of the feelings we get from the elder son's response. The question is, how long had he felt this way? Did his feelings begin as he accepted his role as the eldest son and lived the life expected of him? When did he decide he deserved more than anyone else and, moreover, deserved to be honored for doing the right thing? When did doing the right thing become such a burden to him? When did doing the right thing move from doing it out of love to doing it because of duty? When did he come to resent the father's love for his younger son, believing that it somehow diminished the father's love for him?

Questions:

What similarities did the younger son and the elder son share?

How do you view the elder son's words to his father?

Just as the younger son was returning from the shadow of the valley of death, we find the elder son was also living in the dark shadows—the shadows of resentment, burden, hurt, and anger.

Remember, Jesus is speaking to the gathered Pharisees and law experts. Those who lived "by the books and the law" did not know how to live by the spirit of either. We are often at this juncture where we, too, want to be pleasing to our Father, God, and to be good and virtuous and avoid the pitfalls of sin and temptation; and yet, we are so entrapped by the doing that we become like Pharisees and lose the heart (love) of the Spirit. Subsequently, our being good and obedient, hardworking, and self-sacrificing becomes something for which we expect to be rewarded, praised, and recognized.

In essence, we have stopped doing simply out of our love for God and the joy that comes from that relationship. Instead, we have set up a subliminal merit system for God's grace and forgiveness: "If I do this, then God will do that." We often develop unspoken—and sometimes spoken—criteria under which we think God should forgive us and others. The problem with the merit forgiveness system we create is God does not operate in it. The father in the parable did not operate within such a system either.

The Pharisees and law experts believed and lived much as we do today in our culture. Our culture continues to promote a merit-based system that operates under the philosophies of "work hard and you'll succeed," "do the right things and right things will be done unto you," and "play by the rules and you'll win." From an ethical, moral, and legal standpoint, for the most part, there is nothing wrong with such a system. And maybe that is why we can empathize so readily with the feelings of the elder son. But what this parable teaches us is that we can do all those legal, ethical, and moral things, but without the love of God flowing through us, we may set boundaries that provide no room for love, grace, and mercy.

Questions:

Are there times when you feel you must accomplish something (merit) to gain God's love for you?

Have you ever resented others' successes, especially when it seems they get lucky breaks or do not "play by the rules?"

How difficult is it for you to forgive others for their seemingly wayward behavior because you feel they are undeserving?

The Father

This is a story of scandalous grace, grace that defies all earthly rules and conventions. When the father ran out to greet his son, there were no hoops, clauses, or stipulations for the younger son. Instead, the father displayed one of the fruits of the spirit—pure joy. His son had come home, and the father seemed to put the past behind them in the hope of what was ahead.

My favorite verse in this parable is 15:20: "So he got up and went to his father. While he was still a long way off, his father saw him and was moved with compassion." Even though the younger son was still a long way off, the father saw him and had compassion. I love the imagery of a father out every night watching and waiting for his wayward child to return home. He had allowed his son to leave because of his desire to do so, but he was ever watchful for his return. No doubt in his return, the son looked nothing like he had when he left. Remember, he had been working with the pigs!

I think this scripture is significant in that the story doesn't tell us that the younger son was yet spiritually where he needed to be; he was a long way off, but upon his return home, the father welcomed him with open arms anyway. He does the same for the elder son, who is also a long way off spiritually, even though he stayed home. Some have suggested perhaps the parable should be called "The Return of the Two Lost Sons."

The Closing

We love a God who does not make performance or perfection a criterion of his love for us. We love a God who forgives each of us by his mercy and grace, though none of us—elder or younger son—deserve it. Whoever we are, whatever we have or have not done, we are welcomed home.

The parable is left, like several, with an open ending. How does the story end? We might ask: Does the younger son truly repent and take his place back in the family? Does the older brother recognize his own waywardness, forgive his brother, and experience joy as the father did? Do those listening to the story recognize themselves in the parable and draw closer to God?

Perhaps this parable is open-ended to allow us to find ourselves in the story. I believe I have been—and you have been—represented in all three main figures of the story. We may have found ourselves in the story when:

- Like the younger son, we have strayed far from home, thinking there was another way that was easier, more fun, or less dutiful than the one in which we live and allowed us not to have to think of anyone but ourselves.

- We think there is no return because we cannot come back until we are fully clean.

- Like the older son, we hide in the resentment of others who seem to receive blessing upon blessing, though, in our opinion and judgment, they are undeserving.

- We think we should receive more than others because our actions are more meritorious than others.

- We do not offer compassion to others whose walk differs from ours.

- We cannot forgive what seems to us to be the unforgivable.

- Like the father, we welcome back those who do not deserve the welcoming, but we do so anyway.

- We look with compassion upon those who are lost.

- We offer forgiveness.

- We receive God's mercy and grace and, in turn, offer others the same.

Yes, we have been all three characters in the story at different points in our lives. Ultimately, this story is our story as we, too, have lived life in the shadows. The shadow of selfish living, the shadow of resentful living, and the shadow of hiding from God as we feel we do not deserve God's grace, mercy, or love. We come to recognize that it is ONLY by the grace of God that we continue to live and breathe and have our being. And it is in that grace we find hope as we seek God's help to come out of the shadows and fully come home to God.

Reflection Questions

Before our lesson began, with whom did you most identify in the story?

After the lesson, with whom do you hope to most identify in the story?

What new ideas, learnings, and/or information did you gain from looking again (or for the first time) at this scripture?

What does this parable and others tell us about the reasons God rejoices?

When you look at the main characters in the parable, who do you most want to strive to be?

Additional Resources:

For more reflections on this parable or a deeper understanding of how first-century Jews would have seen the story, I recommend these two texts:

The Return of the Prodigal Son: A Story of Homecoming by Henri J. M. Nouwen (Image Books, Doubleday, 1992).

Short Stories by Jesus by Amy-Jill Levine (Harper One Publishing, 2015).

Lesson 3

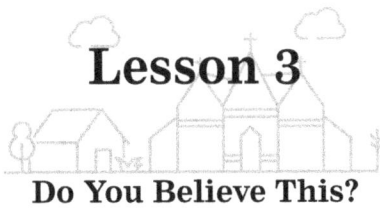

Do You Believe This?
Lesson by Grady Winegar

About the lesson writer:

Grady Winegar served the Holston Conference of the United Methodist Church for forty-four years as Pastor, District Superintendent, Conference Secretary, and Director of Clergy Services. He received a scholarship to pursue a Master of Theology from Duke Divinity School with a major in Preaching the Gospel of John. Preaching is his joyous passion.

Scripture Lesson
John 11

> *Jesus said to her, "I am the resurrection and the life.*
> *Those who believe in me, even though they die, will live,*
> *and everyone who lives and believes in me will never die.*
> *Do you believe this?"*

John 11:25-26

My First Sermon

Every preacher has a story about their first sermon. I recall the story of one young preacher who described how he got up, poured his heart out, and sat down abruptly in a full sweat. He looked at his watch and discovered that he had told everything he knew in less than four minutes. His delivery was shaky but mercifully short!

At the opposite extreme, my first sermon was sixty-five years ago. I was sixteen. Shortly after I was licensed to preach at the Big Stone Gap District Conference, my pastor, Rev. John Meyers, asked me to preach at my home church, Prospect Methodist, in Yuma, Virginia. My sermon was "How to be Happy," based on part of Psalm 34. I am certain the congregation was happy when I finally finished after forty-five minutes! It was unmercifully long, but God used it anyhow to get the attention of a young adult, my neighbor and school bus driver, Jimmy Haynes. I gave an altar call, and Jimmy knelt at the altar, where he trusted Jesus for his salvation.

In James Insight's memoir, *I Turned My Collar Round,* he tells the story of his first sermon in his first parish. On the first day on the job, he opened his mail to find a letter advertising a sermon service that promised to send him a fresh sermon every week for a fee. The envelope included a sample sermon, ready to preach. He wadded it up with indignation and threw it in the waste basket. All week, he struggled to come up with his first sermon. He was bone dry. Finally, in desperation, he plunged into the waste basket late on Saturday night, dug out the sample sermon, smoothed the wrinkled pages, and promised himself, "just this once."

Sunday morning, he grabbed the congregation's attention with the opening sentence: "Ten minutes after you're dead, where will you be?" He then preached the full sample sermon. He felt very guilty when several folks filed by after the service to welcome him and to say, "Good sermon, preacher." For evening worship, James had invited a seminary classmate to preach. His friend was the academic star of his class who aced Hebrew, Greek, and theology. The guest preacher went into the pulpit, fiddled with his notes, adjusted his tie, pulled his glasses down to the end of his nose, glared over them at the congregation, and bellowed, "Ten minutes after you're dead, where will you be?" He continued to preach the exact same mail-order sermon the folks had heard from their new pastor that morning![9]

The Signs of Jesus

Despite the preachers' embarrassment and the congregation's long suffering, this is an important question, isn't it? Where will we be ten minutes after we are dead? Is this all there is? Does death have the last word? Is there something more? Today, as we consider these questions, we turn to the Gospel of John and the signs (John's special word for miracles) and to Jesus' "I am" sayings. John has seven miracle stories of Jesus, which are called signs. These signs point beyond themselves to who Jesus is. Jesus changes water into wine; he heals the official's son who is at death's door. Jesus enables a man who has been an invalid for thirty-eight years to walk; he feeds the five thousand. Jesus

---

[9] James Insight, *I Turned My Collar Round* (Herbert Jenkins, 1956).

walks on water and heals a man born blind. The seventh sign is the raising of Lazarus from the dead, the ultimate sign of who Jesus is.

John's Gospel also has seven unique "I am" sayings of Jesus: I am the door; I am the Good Shepherd; I am the Way, the Truth, and the Life; I am the True Vine. Three of the "I am" sayings are joined with signs. When Jesus feeds the five thousand, Jesus says, "I am the bread of life." When he heals the man born blind, he says, "I am the light of the world." When he raises Lazarus from the dead, he says, "I am the resurrection and the life." Seven signs; seven "I ams." Seven is the perfect number, the full revelation of who Jesus is.

The Lazarus sign is the most magnificent, not just for what it did for Lazarus or the grieving sisters, Martha and Mary. It is wonderful because it points beyond itself to the glory of God present in Jesus now and to the final glory to be revealed in the cross and resurrection. The Lazarus episode is an epiphany, a revealing of who Jesus is. It is an epiphany, a showing forth of the glory and power of Jesus, who commands, "Lazarus, come out!" It is an epiphany, a manifestation of the One whose voice calls joy out of sorrow, delight out of despair, life out of death.

Look at Jesus' conversation with Martha. Jesus loved Martha, Mary, and Lazarus. He was often in their home at Bethany, just outside Jerusalem. Now Lazarus was seriously ill. The sisters sent word to Jesus, who was across the Jordan River, having escaped from enemies in Judea who wanted to stone him. When Jesus heard that Lazarus was ill, he lingered there for two more days, saying that it was for the glory of God. Then Jesus told the disciples that Lazarus was dead and that he was glad he was not there because they could now believe when they saw him in action.

When they arrived back in Bethany, Lazarus had already been in the tomb for four days. That is an important detail. The Jewish practice was for the body to be buried on the day of death. They did not do embalming like in Egypt; they just anointed the body with fragrances and wrappings. Further, they believed that the soul hovered around the body in the grave for three days after death. Then the soul left the body forever. "Four days" points to the reality and finality of Lazarus' death. Martha said to Jesus, "Lord, if you had been here, my brother would not have died. But even now, I know that God will give you whatever you ask of him."

That is complaint and confidence in one breath! Jesus says to Martha, "Your brother will rise again." Martha replies, "I know that he will rise again in the resurrection on the last day." The Pharisees had taught about a resurrection at some future time. Martha probably knew that. She wanted something more. Then Jesus gave Martha the ultimate "I am" saying: "I am the resurrection and the life. Those who believe in me, even though they die, will live, and everyone who lives and believes in me will never die. Do you believe this?"

Martha, do you believe this? Grady, do you believe this? (Your name), do you believe this? That is the key question in the Lazarus story. Jesus' point-blank question to Martha: "Do you believe this?" *Believing* is the big word in John's Gospel. It is not just any belief, but belief in Jesus. Martha's response is the most astounding affirmation of faith anyone can make. She calls him "Messiah, the Son of God." Martha believed. That's the key to John's Gospel.

John opens his Gospel by writing: "All who received him, who believed in his name, he gave power to become children of God"(John 1:12). John 3:16 proclaims, "For God so loved the world that he gave his only Son, that everyone who believes in him may not perish but may have eternal life." Jesus later says to the disciples: "Whoever believes in the Son has eternal life" (John 3:36). In John 6:40, Jesus says to a crowd, "This is indeed the will of my father that all who see the Son and believe in him may have eternal life."

Later, Jesus says to some of his opposition, "Whoever believes has eternal life (John 6:47). Very significantly, Jesus said to Thomas after the Resurrection: "Have you believed because you have seen me? Blessed are those who have not seen me and yet come to believe" (John 20:29). That's the Easter beatitude for each of us. Finally, John declares the purpose of his Gospel: "Now Jesus did many other signs in the presence of his disciples, which are not written in this book. But these are written so that you may come to believe that Jesus is the Messiah, the Son of God, and that through believing you may have life in his name" (John 20:30-31).

Martha believed. In his conversation with Martha, Jesus became the focus of concern rather than Lazarus. The issue is Christology. Who is the Christ to me? When we settle that question, things begin to change. Tragedies and traumas may still come our way, but we know they do not have the last word. Even death does not have the last word for those who believe the One who says, "I am the resurrection and the life."

Now, it is Mary's turn. Like Martha, she complains, "If only you had been here." Mary kneels at the feet of Jesus, weeping. The mourners gathered around Mary were also weeping. Jesus was greatly disturbed and deeply moved. Jesus wept. He wept with a great heart of compassion and empathy. As the Scottish preacher A. J. Gossip noted, "The sisters and Lazarus had a small place in Scripture, but a large place in Jesus' heart."

Does Anybody Care?

Sometimes, when we are hurting, we wonder if anybody cares. Does anybody share our grief? The tears of Jesus remind us that Jesus cares. In 2011, Ottalee and I were in Oklahoma City for the annual meeting of the General Commission on Archives and History. We had the opportunity to see the memorial built on the site of the Murrah Federal Building, which was bombed in April 1995. There is a large reflecting pool, lots of grass, and 168 chairs of metal and glass, memorializing by name each of the victims of that horrendous act of terrorism. There is a remarkable nine-foot statue of Jesus with his left hand clenched over his heart and his right hand covering his face, which is turned slightly away from the place where the terror struck. The words at the base of the statue read simply, "And Jesus wept." These words reveal so much about Jesus. Here is God with a broken heart. Here is the Lord of the Universe with tears. He knows our suffering, our disappointments, our sorrow, and our grief. He has walked in our shoes and lived in our flesh. In all our trials, he is there for us and here with us.

We find ourselves in John's Gospel. The story of Mary, Martha, and Lazarus has our names written all over it. We have hope in Christ, who is the resurrection and the life. He speaks to us as he did to his Bethany friend, "Lazarus, come out." Lazarus shuffled his way out, a sign that Jesus is indeed the resurrection and the life. The Voice that called Lazarus from the dead is the Voice we yearn to hear. Amid the death of our fondest hopes and dreams, He calls us to life. His Word is powerful; he speaks, and it happens. He calls us by name. His Word gives life. Resurrection is now. Eternal life begins now. Whoever lives and believes in him shall never die. Do you believe this?

Do you see the irony in this scene? The road to Easter runs through a cemetery. Jesus gives life to Lazarus as a sign of the life he offers to all who believe in him. But it cost Jesus his life. In the raising of Lazarus, Jesus signed his own death warrant. Because of Lazarus, so many people believed in Jesus that the religious authorities immediately began planning to put both Lazarus and Jesus to death. How ironic is the statement by the High

Priest, Caiaphas, "It is expedient that one man should die for the people, that the whole nation should not perish." Politically true, yes, but also profoundly theologically true.

A few days before the Passover, Jesus returned to the home of Mary, Martha, and Lazarus. They gave a dinner for Jesus. Martha served. Lazarus was seated with Jesus. Mary took a pound of costly perfume and anointed Jesus' feet, wiping his feet with her hair. Judas Iscariot protested that it was an extravagant waste of three hundred denarii, almost a year's wages for a day laborer. Jesus said, "Leave her alone, she bought it that she might keep it for the day of my burial." Jesus was now anointed and prepared to take on the cross, death, and the tomb. Jesus died on the cross, the ultimate sign of extravagant grace, and he arose from the grave so that all Marys, Marthas, and Lazaruses—all of us—might have eternal life, a life that matters here and now and forever!

Do you believe this?

Reflection Questions

How does the story of Lazarus make you feel as you think about your future?

Where do you see yourself in the stories of Lazarus, Mary, and Martha?

Lesson 4

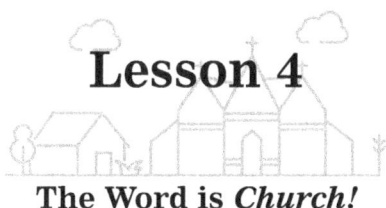

The Word is *Church!*

Lesson by James Bailes

About the lesson writer:

Dr. Jim Bailes is a retired United Methodist pastor who sought to integrate teaching fully in congregational ministry. He authored and taught Bible studies on local, district, and annual conference levels and in a state prison. He also authored the Holston Conference study, *Turning Hearts Toward Children.*

Scripture Lesson
Matthew 16:13-20

> *Now when Jesus came into the district of Caesarea Philippi, he asked his disciples, "Who do people say that the Son of Man is?" And they said, "Some say John the Baptist, but others Elijah, and still others Jeremiah or one of the prophets." He said to them, "But who do you say that I am? Simon Peter answered, "You are the Messiah (or the Christ), the Son of the living God." And Jesus answered him, "Blessed are you, Simon son of Jonah! For flesh and blood has not revealed this to you, but my Father in heaven. And I tell you, you are Peter, and on this rock I will build my church, and the gates of Hades will not prevail against it. I will give you the keys of the kingdom of heaven, and whatever you bind on earth will be bound in heaven, and whatever you loose on earth will be loosed in heaven." Then he sternly ordered the disciples not to tell anyone that he was the Messiah.*

Matthew 16:13-20 (NRSVUE)

As theologian Dietrich Bonhoeffer once preached:

> *There is a word that when a Catholic hears it kindles all his feelings of love and bliss; that stirs all the depths of his religious sensibility, from the dread and awe of the Last Judgement to the sweetness of God's presence; and that certainly awakens in him the feeling of home; the feeling that only a child has in relation to its mother, made up of gratitude, reverence and devoted love; the feeling that overcomes one when, after a long absence, one returns to one's home, the home of one's childhood.*
>
> *And there is a word that to Protestants has the sound of something infinitely commonplace, more or less indifferent and superfluous, that does not make their heart beat faster; something with which a sense of boredom is so often associated, or which at any rate does not lend wings to our religious feelings—and yet our fate is sealed if we are unable to attach a new or perhaps a very old meaning to it. Woe to us if that word does not become important to us soon again, does not become important in our lives.*
>
> *Yes, the word to which I am referring to is Church, the meaning of which we have forgotten and the nobility and greatness of which we propose to look at today.*[10]

Indeed, the word is "Church." The word is Jesus' word. Perhaps (and hopefully) our word. Bonhoeffer describes two greatly contrasting attitudes toward Church. He contrasts what he perceived at the time to be a Catholic reverence for the Church with a Protestant (and he spoke as a Protestant) waning in Church appreciation. Bonhoeffer speaks ominously that "our fate is sealed" if Christians do not regain a biblical understanding of the

---

[10] Dietrich Bonhoeffer, preaching in Barcelona, Spain, July 29, 1928, as quoted in Eberhard Bethge, *Dietrich Bonhoeffer: A Biography* (Fortress Press, 2000).

identity and mission of Church. He evokes the persistent biblical warning of "woe." Much more ominously, we remember Bonhoeffer's warning being tragically disregarded and fulfilled as the German national church, some of the Roman Catholic church, and other fellowships sold their souls to Adolf Hitler, Nazism, the Third Reich, nationalistic idolatry, violence, and murderous racism leading to nothing less than World War II, the Holocaust, and the deaths of millions. History's witness: The church failed to be the Church with horrific results!

Questions for Our Hearts and Minds:

Do you agree with the preceding statements regarding the German church in the 1930s and 1940s?

Did the church in the time and place forsake its Christ-given identity and mission for worldly power and security?

Bonhoeffer's statement is ever relevant. The importance of the Church in modern society seems to have waned significantly in the past half-century.

Thus, this lesson. Thus, hearing again Jesus' words about that word, his word, "Church."

The Text: Following Jesus and the Disciples

Jesus is in the midst of his public ministry. Jesus has evoked all types of responses before and in the aftermath of his birth and all throughout his public ministry. He asks the disciples what they have seen and heard and how people are responding to him. The disciples answer with quite flattering answers: Jesus is variously identified with John the Baptist, Elijah, Jeremiah, or one of the prophets. The disciples omit other less-than-flattering responses: Beelzebul, Prince of Demons, blasphemer.

Jesus then asks another question, THE question: "Who do YOU (disciples) say that I am?"

Question for Our Hearts and Minds:

Who do we say Jesus is?

Who is Jesus to us?

Peter responds immediately as he so often does: "You are the Messiah/the Christ (different Greek words in different manuscripts yet meaning the same), the Son of the Living God!" Jesus, in turn, responds immediately: "Blessed are you, Simon of Jonah!" Jesus blesses and affirms Simon Peter and his response. This is indeed Jesus' identity tied to Jesus' mission! Jesus is the

Messiah/the Christ, God's anointed One, the Son of God. Jesus continues, "And I tell you, you are Peter, and on this rock I will build my church" (Matthew 16:18).

Questions for Our Hearts and Minds:

How do we take Jesus' word to Peter?

How is Peter the rock of the Church? Is it Peter, the person, as some thought? Or is it Peter's confession of faith that Jesus is the Messiah/the Christ?

The Word—Jesus' Word

Jesus introduces the word "Church." "Church" is mentioned only in the New Testament Gospels in Matthew 16:18 and Matthew 18:15. We look closely here at the word, Jesus' word.

The Greek word for "Church" is *ekklesia*. The word was commonly used in the Graeco-Roman world. *Ekklesia* primarily meant a public social gathering. There were various types of *ekklesia:* public hearings, political events, and economic comings together. Public, not private. Social, not individual. Jesus claims *ekklesia* as part of his Kingdom ministry with profound implications: Disciples of Jesus are disciples together, in fellowship, in community.

Questions for Our Hearts and Minds:

Where do we encounter this in the law and prophets' faith in which Jesus was raised?

Where do we find this in Jesus' own life and ministry?

Where and how do we find this in post-Easter Jesus believers at Pentecost in Acts 2?

Do we believe the Church is vital and necessary for following and serving Jesus?

What has been the spiritual impact of Church involvement in our faith lives?

What has been the impact of contemporary individualism on individuals and the Church?

John Wesley affirmed personal faith/holiness and social faith/holiness. By *social holiness,* he meant following and serving Jesus together, in community. Wesley wrote, "Faith that does not begin in the individual does not begin. Faith that ends in the individual ends." The early Methodist movement developed from small group gatherings called class meetings—or society meetings or bands—as well as in worship and mission. *Life Together* is considered by many to be among Dietrich Bonhoeffer's most profound writings. In it, Bonhoeffer describes the Christian life as life together.

The word *ekklesia,* Jesus' word, can be taken apart: *Ek* and *klesia.*

- Ek is a common preposition meaning "from" or "out of."

- Klesia comes from the root meaning "to be called."

- The word taken apart means "called out or from."

- That is, the Church is called. The Church is called together out or from the world to be sent back into the world.

Remembering Others in the Bible who were Called

Abram/Abraham: "Go from your country and your kindred and your father's house to the land that I will show you. I will make of you a great nation, and I will bless you, so that you will be a blessing" (Genesis 12:3).

Moses: "So come, I will send you to Pharaoh to bring my people, the Israelites, out of Egypt" (Exodus 3:10).

49

Joshua: "Now proceed to cross the Jordan, you and all this people, into the land that I am giving to them, the Israelites" (Joshua 1:2).

Gideon: "Go in this might of yours and deliver Israel from the hand of Midian" (Judges 6:14).

Isaiah: "Whom shall I send, and who will go for us?" Isaiah responds—was there any other human around?— "Here I am; send me!" (Isaiah 6:8).

Jeremiah: "Before I formed you in the womb I knew you, and before you were born I consecrated you; I appointed you a prophet to the nations" (Jeremiah 1:5).

Mary: Gabriel speaking for God: "You will conceive in your womb, and bear a son, and you will name him Jesus" (Luke 1:11).

Jesus to his disciples: "Come, follow me" (Matthew 4:19).

The risen Jesus in what we call the Great Commission:

"Go therefore and make disciples of all nations, baptizing them in the name of the Father and of the Son and of the Holy Spirit, and teaching them to obey everything that I have commanded you" (Matthew 28:20).

"Go into all the world and proclaim the Gospel to the whole creation" (Matthew 16:15).

"As the Father has sent me, so I send you" (John 20:21).

"Feed my lambs ... tend my sheep ... feed my sheep ... follow me" (John 21:15-17, 19).

"You shall be my witnesses in Jerusalem, Judea, Samaria, and to the ends of the earth" (Acts 1:8).

Question for Our Hearts and Minds:

When and how has Jesus called you throughout your life? As Church?

The word is "Church," Jesus' word. A community of Jesus' followers called together out of the world to be sent back into the world.

A clincher. Jesus adds a word – "MY": "You are Peter and on this rock I will build MY church" (Matthew 16:18). Jesus does not say "church," "a church," "the church," "some church," and he certainly does not say "your church" or "our church." Jesus says, "MY church."

Jesus claims the Church. Jesus creates the Church, calls the Church, and, perhaps most importantly, claims the Church. As Paul later says, Jesus is the head of the body of Christ, the Church. Jesus is Lord of the Church. Jesus' use of the possessive pronoun "my" cannot be overemphasized: The Church is Jesus' Church, first and foremost and always, Jesus' Church.

My Own Church Experiences (undoubtedly shared by many church leaders over the years)

- I pastored a rapidly growing church. The church grew significantly in people, mission, activities, and outreach. Though everyone had prayed for, worked for, and thanked God for this growth, growth inevitably brought change. A church leader confronted me and said, "This is OUR church!" I tried the best within me—which often is not very good—to witness to Jesus' claim of the Church. (I will say that before I left for another appointment a few years later, the church leader, in his grace, asked me if I remembered that remark. After I hemmed and hawed in admitting to remembering his never-to-be-forgotten remark, he said, "I'm sorry. I'm sorry.")

- A church gathering was discussing a resolution to encourage congregations to study the immigration issue in America biblically, globally, humanely, and legally. During the discussion, a person took the floor and said, "We need to depart from Jesus on this one." A gasp permeated the gathering. The person at least had the awareness and honesty to publicly state that his position was to depart willingly from what he perceived to be Jesus' call on the issue. (The study resolution passed with the help of the person's opposition to it).

- Another church I served had a wonderful annual Christmas pageant. The pageant included a Star of Bethlehem attached to a long allay of pulleys leading the star from "afar" (the back balcony) to Bethlehem (the church altar). An annual highlight of Christmas was seeing the star leading the Magi to the Christ child—except one year when the Magi got ahead of themselves and seemingly paid no attention to the star. The congregation was quite amused as the star, the Star of Bethlehem, frantically flew through the air following the Magi instead of the Magi following the star, a Christmas season parable of the Church expecting God to follow us more than us following God.

Questions for Our Hearts and Minds:

What does it mean for us that Jesus says, "MY" Church?

How is this different from believing and acting as if the Church is my/our church? Do any of these church experiences speak to us?

Do we recall our own such experiences?

What difference would it make in the Church if every thought, every intention, every vision, and every action was led by the realization that the Church is Jesus' Church and not our church?

Perhaps list and compare church issues, questions, possible ministries, etc., according to "my" (Jesus) Church and "my/our" church (ourselves). Are there differences between the two lists? If so, how and why? What might we learn from these contrasts? What such issues do we remember from past years? Racial/ethnic inclusiveness? AIDS sufferers? Community newcomers? Immigrants/refugees? Others?

The Word, Jesus' Word, in Action

Surely we have experiences of the church being the Church. Surely.

More Church Experiences

- A church administrative staff member is an alcoholic in recovery. He thanks God for Alcoholics Anonymous but, as a Christian, is frustrated by what he considers to be the vague references to "A Higher Power" rather than God in Jesus Christ. The person goes to the senior minister and shares a vision of a recovery ministry using the Twelve Steps of Alcoholics Anonymous yet directly connected to the Christian faith and the Bible. The senior minister says, "Go to it!" The God-mission vision was given to Bill Baker, and this affirmation was made by Pastor Rick Warren of Saddleback Church in Lake Forest, California, Los Angeles, leading to the creation of Celebrate Recovery in 1991, now an international ministry blessing millions. This was and is Church. Jesus Church!

- A church member and longtime hospital employee suffered from breast cancer. Her mother and a sister died of breast cancer. Another sister had bone cancer. The church member was told by her oncologist that her best hope was for a basal stem cell transplant, but this procedure was denied by her hospital employer's health coverage. Through it all, her father was hospitalized and critically ill. All he could think about was his daughter's plight. Then, during a pastoral visit, his minister blurted out a word from somewhere (THE somewhere), "We will do it. The church will do it."

- The church was in a transitioning neighborhood lacking the membership and resources of past decades, so this had to be a community/citywide effort. Over the next three months, this now modest-sized and financially resourced church raised eighty thousand dollars to send their beloved member to Duke University Hospital for this treatment! Most of the funds were raised in a single event where this shy, humble woman was serenaded with "Can't You Feel the Love Tonight?" A prominent businessman said this experience renewed his faith in humanity and in the Church!

Question for Our Hearts and Minds:

What experiences have you had of the church being the Church, Christ's Church, something of what Jesus had—and has—in mind for the Church?

A Closing Word

A colleague took his mother, in the late stages of dementia, for a brief drive around the old community. They drove by the lifelong neighborhood. No recognition. They drove past the family homeplace. No recognition. The son was in despair over this until his mother exclaimed, "My church! My church!" Among this dear soul's final earthly recognitions was her church. (And she always realized "her" church was really Jesus' Church). The church, being the Church, had an earthly-eternal impact upon her soul and life.

The Word is "Church." Jesus' Word. Jesus' Church. May it be so for us.

Lesson 5

The Book of Ruth: A Plea for Tolerance
Lesson by Stella Roberts

About the lesson writer:

Stella Roberts is a retired United Methodist elder who served forty-one years in active ministry, pastoring churches in Tennessee, West Virginia, and New Jersey. In addition to local church ministry, she served as a District Superintendent and as Director of Connectional Ministry. Stella enjoys reading, traveling, playing the mountain dulcimer, listening to Old Time music, and walking her German shorthaired pointer, Lolli.

Scripture Lesson
Ruth 4:13-17

> So Boaz took Ruth and she became his wife. When they came together, the Lord made her conceive, and she bore a son. Then the women said to Naomi, "Blessed be the Lord, who has not left you this day without next-of-kin; and may his name be renowned in Israel. He shall be to you a restorer of life and a nourisher of your old age; for your daughter-in-law who loves you, who is more to you than seven sons, has borne him. Then Naomi took the child and laid him in her bosom, and she became his nurse. The women of the neighborhood gave him a name, saying, "A son has been born to Naomi." They named him Obed; he was the father of Jesse, the father of David.

Ruth 4:3-17 (NRSVUE)

The story of Ruth is probably familiar to most of us as a story about the loving relationship between a woman and her daughter-in-law. However, its importance goes far beyond being a love story. If we can understand how the Book of Ruth fits into the Hebrew scriptures as a whole and why Ruth's story is contained in the biblical canon, we can learn that it has something important to say to us today.

The two main characters in the story are Naomi, a Jew, and Ruth, her Moabite daughter-in-law. At this period of their history, the Israelites generally considered Moabites to be despised enemies. Moab would certainly not be a place Jews would choose to go under normal circumstances. But there is famine in Bethlehem, known as the "land of bread" (kind of ironic to have a famine in "the land of bread"), so Naomi, her husband Elimelech, their two sons, and presumably many other Israelites, travel to Moab in search of food. The names of the two sons should give us a clue that there might be trouble ahead. One is named Mahlon (which means "sickness and death"), and the other is named Chilion (which means "annihilation").

Despite all that, they do find food in Moab, and they also find that the Moabites aren't such bad people after all. They are generous, sharing their food with the Israelites and eventually even intermarrying with them. (It's nice to know there is at least one biblical precedent that demonstrates ancient enemies can, indeed, live in peace together.) The family is not in Moab long, however, before Naomi's husband, Elimelech, dies, leaving Naomi with her two sons (the ones with the distressing names). Both of the sons marry Moabite women—Orpah and Ruth, and they settle there for about ten years until both the sons die, leaving three women as widows, without men to care for them (which made them very vulnerable in that day and time).

Naomi decides her best option is to return to Judah to live with her family there. The famine in Judah had ended by this time, and there was plenty of food in "the land of bread," so Naomi urged her daughters-in-law to return to their families in Moab. One daughter-in-law, Orpah, does leave, but Ruth does not, instead responding with the famous words:

> *Do not press me to leave you or to turn back from your company, for wherever you go, I will go, and wherever you live, I will live. Your people shall be my people, and your God, my God. Wherever you die, I will die and there I will be buried. May the Lord do this thing to me and more also, if even death should come between us!*
>
> **Ruth 1:16-17**

Ruth accompanies Naomi home to Judah, journeying specifically to Bethlehem, the home of Naomi's deceased husband, Elimelech. There, they encounter a relative of Elimelech—a wealthy man named Boaz. They glean in Boaz's barley fields, as was customary for widows to do, gathering what the reapers have left behind. And the reapers intentionally leave some behind so others might be fed. Boaz notices Ruth and takes a liking to her. He sees that the fields in which she gleans are especially fruitful, he cautions his men against molesting her, and he allows her access to his employees' water supply. At mealtime, he offers her food. This is indeed special treatment for this Moabite woman.

Naomi, recognizing Boaz's kindness as affection for Ruth and recognizing the need for a more permanent solution for Ruth's future than seasonal gleaning, then plays matchmaker. Says Naomi:

> *"My daughter, I need to seek a home for you, so that it may be well with you. Now here is our kinsman Boaz, with whose young women you have been working. See, he is winnowing barley tonight at the threshing floor. Now wash and anoint yourself, and put on your best clothes and go down to the threshing floor; but do not make yourself known to the man until he has finished eating and drinking. When he lies down, observe the place where he lies; then, go, and uncover his feet and lie down; and he will tell you what to do." And she replied, "All that you tell me I will do."*
>
> **Ruth 3:1-5**

Naomi's directive to Ruth to "uncover his feet and lie down" has strong sexual overtones. Naomi is telling Ruth to engage in risky behavior that would carry a high potential for scandal: to go to a place where she does not belong in the middle of the night to proposition a man who is her social superior. Despite the risk, Ruth does just as Naomi instructs her. When Boaz wakes and finds Ruth lying at his feet, he says:

> *"Who are you?" And she answered, "I am Ruth, your servant; spread your skirt over your servant, for you are next-of-kin." And he said, "May you be blessed by the Lord, my daughter; this last instance of your loyalty is*

better than the first; you have not gone after young men,
whether poor or rich. And now, my daughter, do not be
afraid, I will do for you all that you ask."

Ruth 3:9-11

The upshot of this tryst is that Boaz (the Israelite)
and Ruth (the Moabite) are eventually married. Boaz,
in fact, purchases Ruth and all of Elimelech's property
from Naomi and, at the time of purchase, announces his
intention to marry Ruth. Then comes what is the climax
of this whole story:

> *So Boaz took Ruth and she became his wife. When they*
> *came together, the Lord made her conceive, and she bore*
> *a son. Then the women said to Naomi, "Blessed be the*
> *Lord, who has not left you this day without next of kin;*
> *and may his name be renowned in Israel! He shall be to*
> *you a restorer of life and a nourisher of your old age; for*
> *your daughter-in-law who loves you who is more to you*
> *than seven sons, has borne him." Then Naomi took the*
> *child and laid him in her bosom, and became his nurse.*
> *And the women of the neighborhood gave him a name,*
> *saying, "A son has been born to Naomi." They named him*
> *Obed; he was the father of Jesse, the father of David.*

Ruth 4:13-17

End of story

This beautiful story is about a loving relationship
between a woman and her daughter-in-law, which ends
happily ever after. It is, however, not truly religious
in the traditional sense of that term. Aside from Ruth
becoming a convert to Judaism, there is no deep or
hidden revelation about God here. There is precious
little about the human relationship to God. And there is

no direct reference to how God might be involved in the matters related to the story. What, then, is it doing in the Hebrew Bible? The key question is, why is the story of Ruth included in the Hebrew scriptures?

Remember, Ruth was a judge over Israel. Her story is placed in the canon right after Joshua and Judges. But though her story is set in that time frame of Israel's history (around 1100 BCE), it is generally accepted by biblical scholars that the tale was not told until centuries later. In fact, it has nothing in common with the historical concerns or the literary style of the judges' period and is dated by scholars as post-exilic—that is, coming from a much later time in Israel's history.

According to many scholars, the Book of Ruth was recorded after the period of the judges, after the monarchy was established, after Saul, David, and Solomon ruled as kings in the united kingdom, after the prophets, after the Babylonian captivity and exile, and after the return of the exiles to Jerusalem. After all this history, about seven hundred years, somebody remembers Ruth! "Why?" is extremely important!

Remember that the period of exile was an incredibly difficult time for the people of Israel. The Promised Land was gone. The Davidic line of kings was gone. The Babylonians had dispersed the people into various communities and subcultures, taking away from them everything that was Jewish so they would lose their identities and slowly be absorbed into the culture of their captors. That way, Judaism and its belief in the one God,

Yahweh, would be gone forever. Pretty drastic stuff, this, in a hard, hard time.

Then, in order to maintain the people's identity and faith during the exile, their priests developed the law of God to the nth degree. They held together by following God's law, and, assured by the priests' and prophets' proclamation of a Messiah, they persevered. Times eventually got better because Cyrus of Persia's policy was different. He believed that the way to govern Persia's subject people was to keep them happy. So, rather than wipe out the Hebrews, he let them go home. And under the leadership of Sheshbazaar, the Jews gathered up their things and returned home.

The problem now was that some of their leaders—most notably Ezra (as priest) and Nehemiah (as governor)— still had a kind of siege mentality. They wanted the Jews not only to be identifiable but also to be set apart—even exclusive. They got carried away. Judaism began to draw in upon itself and emphasize pure blood as a necessity.

Ezra and Nehemiah made three demands on the Jews. To be considered an authentic Jew, you had to, one, be loyal to and supportive of the temple; you had to, two, be fully devoted to keeping the law in all its requirements; and three, you had to be of pure Jewish blood. This last point is the crucial one. Seeking to rid Judaism of foreign influences after the exile, Ezra and Nehemiah forced the returning exiles to cast out foreign wives and the children born of those wives. Only those who were of pure stock could consider themselves Jews.

Intermarriages were dissolved then and there and are forbidden in the future.

Considering all this, the Book of Ruth relates to and is critical of this restricted and exclusive understanding of Judaism. Following the return of the exiles and around seven hundred years after her death, someone remembers and retells the story of Ruth, the Moabite, who lived all those many years before. And they did so for a reason!

Hear again the end of the story:

> *So Boaz took Ruth and she became his wife. When they came together, the Lord made her conceive, and she bore a son. Then Naomi took the child and laid him in her bosom, and she became his nurse. And the women of the neighborhood gave him a name, saying, "A son has been born to Naomi." They named him Obed; he was the father of Jesse, the father of David.*

Ruth 4:13-17

The point, finally, is that in the face of the returned Jews' restrictiveness, intolerance, and exclusivity, someone has the good sense to remember Ruth—mother of Obed, grandmother of Jesse, great-grandmother of David. Someone had the sense to remember Ruth, the judge over Israel, Ruth, the MOABITE (the foreigner, the outsider, the immigrant). And in this recollection, the ridiculousness of restricting and making too exclusive the requirements of Judaism is highlighted. If Ezra's and Nehemiah's rules had been in force earlier, David, the great King David, would not have been considered a Jew. That's because David, issued through a Moabite great-grandmother, was not of pure blood.

Since the woman, Ruth, was a Moabite, not an Israelite, the book's effect, if not its purpose, is to create a sympathetic feeling toward foreigners and immigrants who are also protected by Israel's God. So, the suggestion here is that the Book of Ruth is a post-exilic composition based on a much older tale intended to counteract the harsh decrees of Ezra and Nehemiah, which required Hebrew men to divorce their foreign wives and marry only within the covenant community. And the book performs that service admirably. How silly it is, the Book of Ruth implies, to be so restrictive, so exclusive, and so intolerant as to deny David his citizenship within Judaism. To Ezra, Nehemiah, and the many in their stead, Ruth says clearly, The love of God is bigger than you know! The love of God is bigger than any of us knows!

Ezra and Nehemiah wanted to limit God's covenant love to include only those like them—those of pure Jewish blood. And the story of Ruth is remembered and recorded to vehemently counteract that limitation!

Today, I fear the temptation is, similarly, to limit the message of God—the message of God's love and grace—to those who look like we do, who think as we do, who love as we do, who act as we do. Sometimes the divisions are geographical, sometimes racial or ethnic, sometimes political, sometimes gender-based.

But the message scripture proclaims to us today is that we should not fall prey to those temptations. Indeed, we must not fall prey to those temptations. Instead, we should, we can, and we do strongly oppose them—oppose any effort to limit God's love. Christ's church has no requirement pertaining to bloodline. You don't have to be a Southerner or even an American to be welcome in Christ's church. You don't have to be a certain color or have attained a particular economic status. You can be male or female. You can be undocumented, or alien, or a dreamer and still be loved by God and of critical importance to God, and thus, loved and of critical importance to those of us who claim to be followers of God incarnate—Jesus Christ.

You see, the story of Ruth is, in reality, a story of tolerance, a story of inclusiveness, a story of love without limits. And the message of the Book of Ruth in Hebrew scriptures is tolerance.

It's important, though, to clarify what "tolerance" means, for that word has received a bad rap among some circles today. Unfortunately, tolerance has been equated with apathy—sitting back in the midst of evil, injustice, discrimination, suffering, and persecution—just accepting all that as "the way things are" and doing little to work for change. That is not at all the message Ruth is conveying. When we look up some dictionary definitions of tolerance, this is what we find:

> Tolerance is a fair, objective, and permissive attitude toward those whose opinions, beliefs, practices, racial or ethnic origins, etc. differ from one's own; Tolerance is freedom from bigotry.[11]

---

[11] https://www.dictionary.com/browse/tolerance.

This is the kind of tolerance I believe the story of Ruth is advocating, for without tolerance, the great King David—in whose lineage the promised Messiah would come—would not have even qualified as Jewish.

So, Ruth was written to oppose intolerance and exclusiveness among the faith community—to oppose bigotry. And that is what we are called to oppose today in the church and in our world.

William Sloane Coffin was the Yale University chaplain in the early seventies and later served as the senior pastor of Riverside Church in New York City. In response to questions of faith, Coffin said:

> The one absolute is love. The integrity of love is much more important than the purity of dogma. I think dogma is a signpost, not a hitching post. It's always pointing beyond itself to God, and my problem with [many today] is they tend to put the purity of dogma ahead of the integrity of love and end up quite loveless in many instances.

Then Coffin explains:

> I think it's fair to say you can build community out of seekers of the truth, but you can't build community out of possessors of truth because they're also possessed of a certain hatred toward those who don't possess the truth, or who possess another truth than theirs.

I think we worship a God of such divine incomprehensibility that to say we speak for God takes more gall than we should probably allow ourselves. In my deepest thoughts and feelings, we can only say this is how I think it ought to be. But love is, to me, the plumb line which will measure these things. Now, if you believe that, you don't have to hang on to absolute truth with a white-knuckle grip. You're available for deeper meanings that may come your way.

Sometimes, thankfully, we do transcend our locks on the truth and our intolerance, and we not only tolerate, but we also go on to dialogue, to genuine acceptance and even appreciation of one another's perspectives, backgrounds, and cultures. We become available for these deeper meanings in life. Not only did Boaz marry Ruth, but through her great-grandson, David, all of Judaism embraced and canonized her. So her message to us is to be tolerant so that acceptance, appreciation, and even love might eventually result and grow into a love without limits.

John Wesley characterized all this so well in his sermon on the catholic spirit. Wesley says:

> I do not mean, "Be of my opinion." You need not. Neither do I mean, "I will be of your opinion." I cannot. Keep you your opinion; I, mine, and that as steadily as ever. You need not even endeavor to come over to me or bring me over to you. I do not desire that. Let all opinions alone on one side and the other. But if thine heart is as my heart, if thou lovest God and all humankind, I ask no more: "Give me thine hand."

In other words, Be tolerant! Love without limits!

Indeed, today, as the Body of Christ, we are called to be an inclusive—not an exclusive—fellowship and community. And today (as we do every day), we witness to that fact as surely as Ruth did.

Lesson 6

The Seven Deadly Sins

Lesson by Bill Kilday

About the lesson writer:

Bill Kilday served for fifty-one years in the Holston Conference of The United Methodist Church. His career included a stint as a District Superintendent and a few years as a YMCA executive. He was pastor of both small and large churches. After retirement, he served as Director of Congregational Development and Stewardship for the conference. He helped train over 125 pastors in the ministry of Financial Management and helped author a manual by the same name. He has written countless articles and lessons on the importance of pastoral leadership in the area of church finances.

Scripture Lesson
Proverbs 6:16-19 (NIV)

> *There are six things the Lord hates, seven that are detestable to him:*
>
> *Haughty eyes,*
>
> *A lying tongue,*
>
> *Hands that shed innocent blood,*
>
> *A heart that devises wicked schemes,*
>
> *Feet that are quick to rush into evil,*
>
> *A false witness who pours out lies,*
>
> *A person who stirs up conflict in the community.*

The idea of the Seven Deadly Sins was developed as early as the fourth century. There is no direct biblical connection, but some reference Proverbs 6:16-19 as a guide to the church's development of the list. The number "seven" has always been a special number to the Hebrew people. There were seven days of creation, including the day of rest. Other references to seven and its multiples of ten are apparent, especially when Peter asks Jesus if followers are to forgive others seven times. Jesus answers with the hyperbole that we are to forgive seventy times seven, which means "always."

The list of these sins became popular and was emphasized by the Church in the twelfth to fourteenth centuries.

Catholics distinguished between "venial" sins and "capital," or "cardinal," sins, also known as "mortal" sins.

A venial sin meets at least one of the following criteria:

- It does not concern a "grave matter," meaning not serious enough to keep one from salvation.
- It is not committed with the full knowledge of the one sinner.
- It is not committed with both deliberate and acknowledged consent.

Venial sins are slight offenses against the law of God in matters of less importance or, in matters of great importance, an offense committed without sufficient reflection or full consent of the will (i.e., the person did not know or understand what they were doing or did not intend to do it). For example, someone asks you, "Where is your son?" You reply, "He is at the ball game." But, in fact, he is at the sports bar and watching the game on TV. You lied, but you thought you were telling the truth. Venial sins weaken the individual but do not remove them from spiritual life or salvation.

Mortal sins are much more serious offenses against the law of God (i.e., willful disobedience of God). These sins are called mortal because they were believed to deprive the sinner of spiritual life and would cause everlasting death and damnation to the soul. Capital sins destroy the life of grace and lead to eternal damnation without the sacrament of confession and contrition.[12]

The Sins:

- Pride
- Greed
- Lust
- Envy
- Gluttony
- Rage
- Sloth

---

[12] It may be of interest at this point to mention how the Catholic church observes the seven sacraments of Baptism, Eucharist, Holy Orders, Confirmation, Reconciliation/Confession, Marriage, and Anointing. Protestant churches generally observe only Baptism and Holy Communion as sacraments because Jesus participated in those two. Some Protestants practice some of the other rites, but not at the level of being sacraments.

Four of the sins are about the human disposition or nature: pride, greed, lust, and envy. These four sins LEAD to actions but are not actions to begin with. The remaining three sins are about behavior or actions: sloth, gluttony, and rage.

PRIDE – "Prince" of All Sins

At its best, pride is our need to feel good about ourselves. To have pride can mean having a "healthy" ego with an appropriate level of self-confidence and awareness of gifts and graces. The concept of "honor" enters somewhere—that is, the honor that leads to such things as honesty and actions we do because of an inherent sense of what is "right."

The sinfulness or downside of pride is being "dishonored" and the subsequent need for revenge or even "vendetta" (more about that later). But pride can also be the need to feel superior to others. It often leads to self-indulgence at the expense of others. The notion that we are better than others leads to the practice of looking down on other people as inferior and treating others with indignation and contempt.

Pride brings classism and caste systems, racism, slavery, nationalism, demonization, hate, distractionism, i.e., war, genocide, and ethnic cleansing. (We can point at the Nazis, but we also have to look at the treatment of enslaved people and the Native Americans in this country.)

Pride can also cause us to deny our self-reality: being in denial about our lack of responsibility or our responsibility for wrongs and misdeeds, making alibis, and lying to avoid blame for deeds and decisions. It can also be braggadocious, calling undue attention to oneself and particularly overestimating self-worth and ability to the point of delusion.

GREED

Greed is the desire for more, and more, and more. It can lead to excessive luxury and opulence. Greed begs the question, "What is enough?"

Jesus condemned greed almost more than any other human trait. We remember what he said about rich people getting into heaven, as in the camel going through the eye of a needle, and what he said about rich people being insensitive to the needs of others in the parable of the rich man and Lazarus. We also think of the conversation with the rich young ruler.

Wealth insulates people from the needs of the not-so-wealthy.

How much is enough?

A story is told of forty exchange students at the airport. They had been told not to take more than forty pounds of luggage. They thought they were allowed fifty pounds, so when their bags were weighed and were all too heavy, they were ordered to cut ten pounds or more or pay a heavy fine. All the bags went on the floor, and all sorts of "necessary" items were transferred to their parents.

Greed causes an insatiable appetite for more. This

appetite is not tempered by need.

There is a big difference between saving for a "rainy day"—or even retirement—and storing up what Jesus would call "treasures on Earth." Remember the character Gordon Gekko in the movie Wall Street with Michael Douglas when he says, "Greed is Good. The evil of greed is when one person or a group of persons hoards resources and thereby denies those resources to others who desperately need them.

There is a story of the man who buried his money in the backyard, and somebody dug it up and stole it. His neighbor reminded him, "You never used it for anything anyway."

The parable of the rich man and building bigger barns is about selfish hoarding and the failure to have compassion or generosity.

LUST

A synonym for lust is *lechery,* which is an inordinate craving for sexual intercourse or activity, often to the point of assuming a self-indulgent and sometimes violent character. It is the inordinate craving for, or indulgence of, the carnal pleasure experienced in the human "organs of generation," according to a medieval definition.

Lust is the obsessive desire for sexual pleasure and is probably the most emphasized, written about, and tantalizing of the Seven Deadly Sins. Certainly, it is the most advertised. Everywhere we look, sex is used to sell and is advertised as a free and easy commodity. Somewhere in California, there is a lust club. People apply, send three pictures, prove their health and character, and pay money. As members, they may attend events, which are occasions to associate with like-minded people. And contrary to some conservative beliefs, we in the modern era did not invent it.

The danger of unbridled and uncontrolled lust is the destruction of culture. Because of lust and without some restraint, the sins of envy and rage can become more prevalent, and murder might be even more common. The obsessive, unbridled practice of lust has brought down more than one kingdom or powerful office.

Jesus said that if we even look at a person with lust, that is equal to committing adultery in our hearts.

ENVY

Another word for envy is *covetousness*. Most of us have some desire for that which we do not have. Envy is akin to greed in some ways. Greed never has enough, and envy always wants what others have. Envy ignores our sufficiency or happiness with what we have and what we are because we see someone who has more or seems to be happier or better off.

Two fishermen were trying their luck in the Gulf Stream in South Florida. They happened into a school of mahi-mahi. After catching several nice specimens, their luck slowed down. One fish would follow the bait almost all the way to the boat as the fishermen reeled in. But while only one fish was interested, no fish would bite the bait. After some time, a second fish showed interest. As soon as there was competition, the two fish went for the bait, stirring up the water. Suddenly, from below, a dozen or more others came up. The frenzy was on. The fishermen started catching fish after fish since the water was stirred. The fish acted almost like humans. As long as no other fish was interested in the bait, it was not alluring. But when others wanted the same thing, the frenzy started. We sometimes want something just because it looks attractive to somebody else.

In NCAA football recruiting ratings, when an athlete has only minor attention from recruiters, other college offers are not forthcoming. But if one major program makes an offer, the recruit's stock goes up, and his rating increases. We all seem to want what others want.

There is a kinship of envy with jealousy. Jealousy is a negative feeling about someone who looks better, has a better life, "gets" more breaks, or we perceive to have more money, possessions, success, pleasure, satisfaction, etc.

Sadly, our economy feeds off envy and, to a similar extent, greed. The advertising industry spends millions to tell us what we want, need, and can't live without and, in the process, uses sex and lust to make the point.

What happens when we quit buying everything in sight? Slow down our eating out? Don't replace our cars, clothes, electronic equipment, etc., as quickly as we used to? Unfortunately, the COVID crisis answered this question for us. Many businesses were forced to close their doors, lay people off, and reduce their offerings.

Envy leads to dislike, dislike to demonizing, demonizing to hate, and hate to murder—which brings us to our next sin.

RAGE

What is the difference between anger and rage?

Anger is usually associated with frustration resulting from a loss of control. At a lesser level, anger can be a simple annoyance. Minor annoyances can be easily left alone. But, a greater or more consistent annoyance can cause a more direct reaction, i.e., speaking out and acknowledging the source of the annoyance. More serious anger comes out of a feeling of being belittled, threatened, or harmed. If anger is allowed to escalate, it can lead to rage.

Rage denotes aggression, where anger is motivated by causing harm to others. It is also characterized by impulsive thinking and a lack of planning. When one experiences rage, it usually lasts until a threat is removed or the person who is the subject of rage is maimed, injured, or killed. It is troublesome that rage seems to be more common in the twenty-first century.

The movie Seven (Morgan Freeman and Brad Pitt) illustrates the contrivance of the perpetrator of several murders to induce rage in one of the investigators. The movie also brings the Hollywood version of the Seven Deadly Sins to the script.

In some cultures, there is the practice of "vendetta." If someone dishonors a person or family, there is a notion that the wrong must be answered as a matter of honor. One dictionary calls vendetta "a prolonged bitter quarrel with or campaign against someone."

Irruptive and Disruptive Anger…Road Rage…Revenge

How does one tell the difference between rage and normal amounts of anger? Anger is explained by a current dissatisfaction in one's life. This amount of anger or frustration is common. Rage, however, is caused by built-up anger from past traumas. These accumulated angry dispositions are locked in our minds and bodies. One can mask rage by appearing overly dominant or by being depressed. Screaming, physical expressions of anger, violence or threats of violence, sulking, manipulation, emotional blackmail, silent smoldering, and anger are used to punish.

Healthy anger is not used to punish, is not violent, and isn't used to intimidate, control, or manipulate. It is expressed, discussed, and moved through. Healthy anger is not stuffed down and ignored (stuffed anger creates resentment and a wealth of physical, mental, and emotional problems).

Healthy anger is not expressed in passive-aggressive and manipulative ways. Rage can easily lead to harm or murder of the person or persons who are subjects of the rage.

GLUTTONY

The word *gluttony* comes from a Latin word meaning to gulp down or swallow.

We may need to ask ourselves whether we eat to live or live to eat. How much is enough?

When we think of gluttony, we think of uncontrolled appetites. (Lust and greed can also be gluttonous.)

Gluttony can be overindulgence and overconsumption of anything to the point of waste. In the Christian tradition, it is considered a sin because of the excessive desire for food, causing its withholding from the needy. Depending on the culture, gluttony can be seen as either a vice or a sign of status. Where food is relatively scarce, being able to eat well might be something to take pride in (although this can also result in a moral backlash when confronted with the reality of those less fortunate). Where food is readily available, it may be considered a sign of self-control to resist the temptation to overindulge.

Thomas Aquinas suggested six ways our eating habits could be considered gluttony:

- Eating too soon
- Eating too expensively (exotic foods)
- Eating too much
- Eating too eagerly
- Eating too daintily
- Eating wildly

A 1998 Purdue University study showed that religious people are more likely to be overweight than non-religious people.[13] Why?

SLOTH

More than other sins, the definition of sloth has changed considerably since its mention as one of the Seven Deadly Sins. It was first called the sin of sadness or despair. Early on, it was described as melancholy: apathy, depression, and joylessness. Being without joy was viewed as a refusal to enjoy the goodness of God and the world God created. Originally, it was described as a spiritual apathy that discouraged the faithful from their religious work. It was associated with sadness, or a feeling of dissatisfaction or discontent, which caused unhappiness with one's current situation.

When Thomas Aquinas selected sloth for his list, he described it as an "uneasiness of the mind," a beginning of lesser sins such as restlessness and instability. Some writers described sloth as being the "failure to love God with all one's heart, all one's mind and all one's soul." It was also considered the middle sin and, as such, was the only sin characterized by the absence or insufficiency of love. (In Dante's famous poem "Purgatorio," the slothful penitents were made to run continuously at top speed.)

Sloth is currently considered the failure to fully use one's talents and gifts. For example, a student

---

[13] https://www.purdue.edu/uns/html4ever/2006/060824.Ferraro.obesity.html

who does not work beyond what is required (and thus fails to achieve their full potential) could be labeled slothful. Today, interpretations are much less rigid and comprehensive than they were in medieval times. We now interpret sloth as being more simply a sin of laziness or indifference, an unwillingness to act, or an unwillingness to care (rather than a failure to love God and his work). For this reason, sloth is now commonly seen as being considerably less serious than the other sins. The dangers are that it might lead to "letting yourself go." It could lead to a "loss of the good benefits of pride" or the allowance of gluttony.

The "Other" Side of the Seven Deadly Sins

Pride can bring positive self-esteem, honor, and, thus, honesty. It can promote good personal habits, sanitation, grooming, healthful lifestyle, graciousness, civility, diplomacy, and many other desirable qualities.

Greed, in small quantities, causes us to desire to better ourselves, save for a "rainy day," and provide for our own needs rather than being a burden on society or family. Greed, in a small way, causes our economic system to work and creates opportunities for businesses and entrepreneurs. John D. Rockefeller, Bill Gates, and Warren Buffett have created jobs of wealth for many and have, by their generosity, provided millions for the good of many causes.

Lust is needed if the human race is to propagate and

continue to reproduce. Without lust, we wouldn't be here. Nor would our children or grandchildren.

Envy is difficult to justify, but without some envy, we probably wouldn't be as inventive or innovative as we are. Without envy, we could become self-satisfied, possibly slothful, and our desire to find a better way to do things could decrease. Envy in small doses is great advertisement.

Rage, or at least its cousin anger, is sometimes justified and productive. Righteous anger leads to redress of wrongs. Jesus exhibited anger at least four times during his ministry:

- Cleansing the temple (Matthew 21:12-17)
- Healing the shriveled hand (Mark 3:1-6)
- The hypocrites (Matthew 23:25-36)
- Peter, when he encouraged Jesus to avoid Jerusalem (Matthew 16:21-23)

Gluttony is, to some degree, necessary. Appetite is a needed human drive so that we will eat.

Sloth, in a minor usage, can be just taking a break, resting, changing gears, seeking recreation and refreshment.

The point is MODERATION, understanding when boundaries are being crossed and moving into INDULGENCE rather than usefulness.

Reflection Questions

Is there such a thing as purposeful anger? Anger at injustice? Anger at violence?

Can you think of times when righteous anger accomplished a good thing?

Can you think of an instance when greed or envy produced good results?

Lesson 7

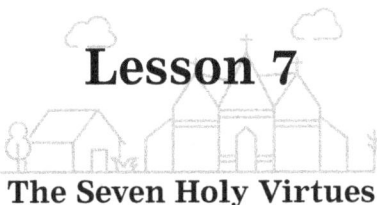

The Seven Holy Virtues

Lesson by Bill Kilday

About the lesson writer:

Bill Kilday served for fifty-one years in the Holston Conference of The United Methodist Church. His career included a stint as a District Superintendent and a few years as a YMCA executive. He was pastor of both small and large churches. After retirement, he served as Director of Congregational Development and Stewardship for the conference. He helped train over 125 pastors in the ministry of Financial Management and helped author a manual by the same name. He has written countless articles and lessons on the importance of pastoral leadership in the area of church finances.

Scripture Lessons:
1 Corinthians 13 and Galatians 5:22-26

> *If I speak in the tongues of mortals and of angels, but do not have love, I am a noisy gong or a clanging cymbal. And if I have prophetic powers, and understand all mysteries and all knowledge, and if I have all faith, so as to remove mountains, but do not have love, I am nothing. If I give away all my possessions, and if I hand over my body so that I may boast, but do not have love, I gain nothing. Love is patient; love is kind; love is not envious or boastful or arrogant or rude. It does not insist on its own way; it is not irritable or resentful; it does not rejoice in wrongdoing, but rejoices in the truth. It bears all things, believes all things, hopes all things, endures*

*all things. Love never ends. But as for prophecies, they
will come to an end; as for tongues, they will cease; as
for knowledge, it will come to an end. For we know only
in part, and we prophesy only in part; but when the
complete comes, the partial will come to an end. When I
was a child, I spoke like a child, I thought like a child, I
reasoned like a child; when I became an adult, I put an
end to childish ways. For now we see in a mirror, dimly,
but then we will see face to face. Now I know only in part;
then I will know fully, even as I have been fully known.
And now faith, hope, and love abide, these three; and the
greatest of these is love.*

1 Corinthians 13 (NRSVUE)

*By contrast, the fruit of the Spirit is love, joy, peace,
patience, kindness, generosity, faithfulness, gentleness,
and self-control. There is no law against such things. And
those who belong to Christ Jesus have crucified the flesh
with its passions and desires. If we live by the Spirit, let us
also be guided by the Spirit. Let us not become conceited,
competing against one another, envying one another.*

Galatians 5:22-26 (NRSVUE)

Having looked at the Seven Deadly Sins, we need to
be reminded that some behaviors and directions can be
desired and practiced instead of the sins. These virtues
were developed out of Plato's Scheme of Education around
330 BCE, so they preceded the Christian era by several
hundred years.

After the first century, these virtues were extended
or amended by Christian writers such as Ambrose,
Augustine, and Aquinas during the beginning of the
Christian era. Ambrose and Augustine were active
in the fourth century, and Aquinas was active in the
thirteenth century.

Four "cardinal" virtues and three "theological" virtues were established. Cardinal virtues are taken from "cardo" or "hinge" because they are "hinges" upon which the door to moral living swings.

Prudence, justice, temperance, and courage were the cardinal virtues. These were understood to be the other side of specific deadly sins.

Theological virtues are those where the emphasis is on the divine being (*theos*, or God). They are not opposites of a vice since it is not considered a vice to have an unlimited amount of faith, hope, and love.

Aurelius Clemens Prudentius wrote an epic poem in 410 CE called "Contest of the Soul." It became popular in the Middle Ages, and the concept of these good virtues and evil vices was commonly accepted throughout Europe. Practicing the virtues was believed to protect people against temptation from the Seven Deadly Sins. Each virtue has a counterpart, so each virtue presents itself as a counterpart to a particular sin.

We will look at the Seven Holy Virtues taken from these early values.

HUMILITY

We begin with *humility,* which is the other side of pride. Humility is seen in bravery and modesty. It demonstrates selflessness and respectfulness and emphasizes giving credit to others. It is not self-aggrandizing.

A Useful "Side Story"

Two college friends were walking on campus together. One was a well-rounded student, active in athletics, clubs, and social events. The other was a star athlete, student body president, and a popular person. As they walked, the second said to the first, "I try to be helpful to people when I can. I try not to take myself too seriously. I try to be humble. As a matter of fact, one of the things I am proudest of is my humility."

The other student stopped in his tracks and said, "Do you hear what you just said? How can you be proud of being humble?"

The student who made the comment had not thought through the irony of his comment.

In the 1970s, there was a popular emphasis on a form of psychotherapy called transactional analysis developed by psychiatrist Eric Berne. The fascination was based on a book by Thomas A. Harris called *I'm OK – You're OK.*[14]

The book describes four possible life positions most people fit into. The first position is "I'm NOT OK – You're OK." In this position, a person feels somewhat inferior while viewing others as well-adjusted and confident. According to Berne, most of us feel this way for the majority of our lives. When we are babies and children, everyone is more capable and knowledgeable than we are, and we learn to be dependent on the care

---

[14]   Thomas A. Harris, I'm OK – You're OK (Harper & Row, 1967).

and wisdom of these "others."

- When have you ever felt this way?

The second life position is "I'm not OK – You're Not OK." This comes about when a person learns of their own inabilities, but they are also aware of the failures and shortcomings of others. This person has possibly been abused and feels animosity toward the abusers. Therefore, no one is to be trusted or admired.

The next position is "I'm OK– You're Not OK." In this scenario, the person may overcome the feelings of inadequacy by determination but sees others as undeserving of trust and despises them. Such figures as Al Capone, Hitler, and many other tyrants of history may be included in this category.

- Does anyone feel this way about any other person? Why?

The final position is "I'm OK – You're OK." This is obviously the most desirable position wherein a person feels reasonably confident and good about themselves and feels OK and accepting of others as well.[15]

True humility can come about when we attain this life position. We have healthy self-respect, accept others, and try to live harmoniously with everyone. This would seem to be the position Jesus exemplified and taught. God gives

---

[15] ibid.

us the grace to be the confident servant we are created to be and the compassion to treat others as equals, with respect and appreciation.

Humility is not overly self-critical but realistic and honest about self and others. Back when the Super Bowl was in its first years, a brash quarterback on the underdog team stated, "I guarantee we'll win the game." He was highly criticized and disparaged for this remark. Yet, when the game was played, his team won, and he was vindicated. As an old sportswriter once said, "It ain't braggin' if you can do it!"

Jesus praised "meekness" in the Beatitudes. The word "meek," which comes from Greek, is often misinterpreted in present-day English. The Greek philosopher Aristotle defined meekness as a virtue because it is a balance between two extremes. It stands between becoming angry at the wrong things for the wrong reason and not becoming angry at anything. It is the balance between being reckless and being cowardly. Jesus exhibited strength with appropriate anger on several occasions, most notably when he chased the money changers from the temple.

CHARITY

Charity, which is on the other side of greed, is illustrated by generosity, a willingness to give of one's resources. It displays a nobility of thought and action. Charitable persons have a heart for sharing, regardless of need; i.e., charity is not motivated by seeing a need but by having a generous heart. Charity gives without regard to reward or forced demand. It is not limited to sharing material possessions, although it does do that; it also includes giving time, energy, and ability. One may think of the Amish style of cooperative living.

In Acts 2:43-47, we read of the early followers of Christ sharing their lives completely. They had all things in common. They sold their possessions and gave the proceeds to those who were in need. They demonstrated charity and generosity.

One may also think of John Wesley, who was determined to live on only what was necessary and give everything else away. We remember St. Francis of Assisi, who took the vow of poverty and started an order of the priesthood to exemplify poverty.

Then there is Mother Teresa, who avoided fame and honor to live among and minister to the sick and dying.

In a "side story," it is said that Mother Teresa was visited by a short-term missionary who witnessed her work among the destitute in the worst of conditions. Upon completing her time with Mother Teresa, the lady said, "I wouldn't do what you are doing for a million dollars." Mother Teresa replied, "Neither would I."[16]

Mahatma Gandhi, who sacrificed a world-class career to lead his country to independence through self-sacrifice, provides us with yet another model of charity and generosity.

---

[16] americamagazine.org/faith/2017/02/02/what-mother-teresa-wouldnt-do-million-dollars

• Can you think of others who may have lived simply and been examples of generosity and charity?

CHASTITY

Chastity, which is the other side of lust, is defined by wholesomeness, purity, courage, and self-denial. The root word comes from "Castus" meaning "pure." Originally, chastity was synonymous with "virginity." It was believed to include the practice of celibacy and the expectation of abstinence from all sexual activity. It was also recognized as faithfulness in marriage, though in many cultures, women were held to higher standards than men (maybe because men made the rules?). In medieval times, the use of the chastity belt for women was practiced. When men went to fight the Crusades, or on other long excursions, wives were expected to wear these devices to prevent them from adultery.

For the Jewish culture, the genealogical issue, as in the progeny of children, was of supreme importance—especially one's paternal genealogy—so women needed to be particularly "chaste" or faithful, so there could never be any doubt as to the father's identity.

KINDNESS

Kindness is the opposite of envy and is noted for satisfaction, friendship, and sympathy. Being kind to those with whom we are sympathetic or friends is natural and easy. When we are satisfied with our state of being and comfort level, we can be kind toward others more easily. While envy wishes ill for others, kindness wishes for and acts out goodness. Kindness, therefore, is an act, more than a demeanor. It is the act or state of "being kind" and doing kind things and is noticed by charitable behavior and demonstrates a mild disposition, with tenderness and concern for others.

The Jewish Talmud claims that "deeds of kindness are equal in weight to all the commandments." Paul defines love as being "patient and kind" (1 Corinthians 13). Paraphrasing Aristotle's Rhetoric, love is one of the emotions defined as helpfulness towards someone in need. It is done not in return for anything, nor for the advantage of the helper himself, but for that of the person helped.

Kindness is also listed as one of the nine "Fruits of the Holy Spirit" in Galatians 5:22-24. As he lists these, Paul writes, "Against these, there is no law."

In regard to the word sympathy, we are more likely to practice kindness toward those with whom we are sympathetic or "feeling with." For instance, our sympathy is increased for a person in pain, trouble, or distress. When we "feel" their condition with them, we are more inclined to practice kindness toward them. On the other hand, if we envy them, we are not inclined to offer kindness.

DILIGENCE

Diligence, or *zeal,* is the other side of sloth. We use adjectives like persistence, effort, attentiveness, and alertness to describe diligence. It is demonstrated by care in one's actions and worth and involves budgeting one's time and monitoring activities to guard against uselessness about how we spend or use our time.

Let us momentarily compare our age with that of many productive people of the past. For instance, John Wesley arose around 4:30 a.m. and retired at 9:00 p.m. He would still get around seven-and-a-half hours of sleep. But remember that England had little more than twelve hours of pure daylight for more than six months of the year. It usually got dark by 9:00 p.m. and got light at 4:30 a.m.

Wesley rode on horseback up to a quarter of a million miles, reading during much of that time. He spent time in Georgia around Savannah and St. Simon's Island. He wrote and published volumes of books and tracts and kept a diary, which was to become a work of literature. He translated the Bible into English from three languages. He wrote and preached thousands of sermons, many of which he published. He started innumerable churches, influenced a nation toward moral renewal, and started a "sect" that was to become a major force in religious life in the new American nation and throughout many other countries. Methodism is now one of the fastest-growing faith movements in Korea and Africa.

Before marveling too much (but we should still

marvel), we remember that there was no TV, no movies, few magazines, and very few novels, and those that existed were literary works. There were no Super Bowls or athletic championships. There were no golf courses, bowling alleys, Olympics, water skiing, etc.

Wesley indeed used his time "diligently."

Consider Thomas Jefferson, John Adams, Abigail Adams, Benjamin Franklin, and many other "founding fathers" of our country. They all wrote copiously of life in their diaries, letters, and philosophical treatises. They were diligent in the use of time.

Most great writers, inventors, and statesmen have in common a diligence and persistence that is intentional.

- What if we did not have all the above-listed choices regarding how we use our time? Would we do more diligent things?

PATIENCE

Patience is the other side of rage, or wrath, and is characterized by peacefulness, tolerance, and endurance through moderation. Patience is identified with mercy and forgiveness. It involves resolving conflict through understanding and peaceful negotiation rather than violence. Patience is sometimes combined with meekness (that is, the meekness defined earlier in this lesson. Patience is often associated with weakness or submissiveness, but it is properly understood as peaceful, patient, and kind … gentleness is one of the nine fruits of the Holy Spirit (Galatians 5:22-24).

When Jesus said, "Blessed are the meek," he was referring to those who responded appropriately to the circumstances. He was angry and chased out the money changers—because it was the appropriate response. Meekness is a sign of strength because it does not require violence, bluster, or threatening language and action. It requires a strong sense of "self" without being threatened by other people's perceptions. It is said that a journalist once asked Robert E. Lee's opinion about a general who had spoken critically and harshly of Lee. Lee spoke highly of the general in question, and his interviewer said, "Are you not aware of what he has said about you?" Lee responded, "You didn't ask me what he thought of me. You asked what I thought of him!" That is strength in meekness.

Patience and meekness are nonretaliatory unless retaliation is a last resort. Paul speaks of "love" as not being boastful or self-seeking, rude or arrogant. "Love bears all things," Paul says. That is the proper understanding of meekness and patience as exhibited in this virtue. Paul also says, "I have learned, in whatsoever state I find myself, therewith to be content." That is the patience meant by this virtue.

- When do we need more patience?

TEMPERANCE

Temperance is the other side of gluttony and is characterized by moderation, self-control, and abstention. Self-control is also one of the fruits of the Holy Spirit.

Perhaps this virtue is one of the most important for our generation to practice more intentionally. If you read over the "works of the flesh" listed by the Apostle Paul in Galatians 5:19-22, you will see that these things are not new to this age. But, arguably, there has never been an age so saturated with so many temptations that are so widely publicized and available as this one. Fortunately, Paul adds verses 22 and 23 to demonstrate a better possibility.

The continuing popularity of the theme of crime in movies, TV shows, and literature indicates that there are plenty of temptations to lead people into undesirable actions. When we pray, "Lead us not into temptation," we are asking to have unworthy and dishonorable activities removed from our paths.

The Seven Holy Virtues are to be practiced, while the Seven Deadly Sins are to be avoided.

So, do we participate in a faith based on avoidance or one based on practice? Jesus used "love" as an *active verb*.

For Jesus, love was what you did, not what you felt. Jesus said, Love, do (unto others,) feed, give, clothe, minister, visit. DO was the benchmark in the teachings of Jesus. Toyohiko Kagawa was an influential Japanese pacifist in the early half of the twentieth century. Attributed to him is the quote, "I read in a book that a man named Christ went about doing good. It is disconcerting to me that I am so easily satisfied with just going about."

While the Seven Deadly Sins invade our very nature and we all fall prey in some way to each of them at times, the Seven Holy Virtues give us the guidelines for practicing alternatives to the sins (that, and the love and forgiveness of God).

It is safe to say that if we live in such a way as to produce the Nine Fruits of the Holy Spirit, we can do well.

> Love, joy, peace, patience, gentleness, generosity, faithfulness, kindness and self-control. "Against these, there is no law."

Lesson 8

Faithful Discipleship: Loving and Serving

Lesson by Susan Groseclose

About the lesson writer:

Susan Groseclose serves the Holston Conference of The United Methodist Church as Associate Director of Connectional Ministries for Discipleship and Leadership.

Scripture Lesson
Luke 10:25-42

An expert in the law stood up to test Jesus. "Teacher," he said, "what must I do to inherit eternal life?" He said to him, "What is written in the law? What do you read there?" He answered, "You shall love the Lord your God with all your heart and with all your soul and with all your strength and with all your mind and your neighbor as yourself." And he said to him, "You have given the right answer; do this, and you will live."

But wanting to vindicate himself, he asked Jesus, "And who is my neighbor?" Jesus replied, "A man was going down from Jerusalem to Jericho and fell into the hands of robbers, who stripped him, beat him, and took off, leaving him half dead. Now by chance a priest was going down that road, and when he saw him he passed by on the other side. So likewise a Levite, when he came to the place and saw him, passed by on the other side. But a Samaritan while traveling came upon him, and when he saw him he was moved with compassion. He went to him and bandaged his wounds, treating them with oil and wine. Then he put him on his own animal, brought him to an inn, and took care of him. The next day he took out two denarii, gave them to the innkeeper, and said, 'Take care of him, and when I come back I will repay you whatever more you spend.' Which of these three, do you think, was a neighbor to the man who fell into the hands of the robbers?" He said, "The one who showed him mercy." Jesus said to him, "Go and do likewise."

Now as they went on their way, he entered a certain village where a woman named Martha welcomed him. She had a sister named Mary, who sat at Jesus'sfeet and listened to what he was saying. But Martha was distracted by her many tasks, so she came to him and asked, "Lord, do you not care that my sister has left me to do all the work by myself? Tell her, then, to help me." But the Lord answered her, "Martha, Martha, you are worried and distracted by many things, but few things are needed—indeed only one.[m] Mary has chosen the better part, which will not be taken away from her."

Luke 10:25-42 (NRSVUE)

Thumbs Up or Thumbs Down?

A legal expert tests Jesus by asking, of all the 613 ordinances of Jewish law, "What must I do to gain eternal life?" Basically, he is asking Jesus which law is the greatest. Instead of answering the question, Jesus asks what his understanding of the law is. The legal expert responds with the Great Commandment: "You must love the Lord your God with all your heart, with all your being, with all your strength, and with all your mind and love your neighbor as yourself." Jesus says that his answer is correct, but the legal expert asks for a further interpretation and asks Jesus, "Who is my neighbor?"

Interestingly, in the Gospel of Luke, Jesus responds to the lawyer's question with two stories about loving and serving. We often study each story individually, but if you combine these two stories, they illustrate what is required to love God and neighbor. The first story is the Good Samaritan, followed by the second story about Mary and Martha.

As a group:

As you hear these statements, decide whether you agree or disagree with them. If you agree with the statement, raise your thumb. If you disagree with the statement, point your thumb down. If you are unable to agree or disagree, shake your thumb between up and down.

- I am faithfully growing in love with God and others.

- I look for opportunities to serve others.

- I go out of my way to befriend others, especially those who are different from me or whom I might initially be uncomfortable around.

- Serving others, I often become an advocate working for equity and justice.

- I faithfully dedicate time each day to deepen my relationship with God.

- I spend as much time loving God as I do in serving others.

- There is a correlation between loving God and serving others.

- My deep relationship with God empowers me to readily serve others.

As a group, share your reasons behind agreeing or disagreeing with these statements. What new insights do you gain from others' perspectives?

What's Happening?

Since these two Bible stories are familiar, we often fail to see any new meaning in them for our lives. If you are with a group, create five columns on a whiteboard or piece of newsprint. Title each column using one of these five words: see, hear, smell, taste, feel. Reread the story of the Good Samaritan. Share your answers to these questions with the group:

- What do you see?

- What do you hear?

- What do you smell?

- What do you taste?

- What do you feel?

Write the group's answers under the appropriate column. Next, reread the story of Mary and Martha using the same process.

As you look over the lists, what is something that you had not realized before? How do these new insights enhance or change your reading of these stories?

Who Are You?

Which character do you identify with today? Be careful not to say who you want to be like. Share who you most identify with and why with a partner or with the group.

As a group, conduct a character study using the following discussion questions:

- Why is the reader not given the wounded man's name?

- Why does the gospel writer not include any information about the wounded man?

- When was the last time you were hurting?

- Who surprised you by offering God's love and compassion?

The approximately seventeen-mile, steep, winding road between Jerusalem and Jericho was known to be extremely dangerous. Persons traveling this desert-like road would go from Jerusalem, a semi-dry area, down in elevation to Jericho, a barren, parched area. Even though this was a major thoroughfare, the road was often named the Way of Blood because it was easy for robbers to attack and shed another's blood. Because of the barren conditions, there was no water or shelter close by or any protection against the elements.

Both the Levite and priest were religious men. A person coming upon the wounded man would not have been able to easily avoid him.

- How do you justify or not justify their actions?

- What circumstances or persons do you tend to avoid? Why?

Samaritans, who were half Jew and half Gentile, were hated by Jews. After the Assyrian captivity of the Israelites of the northern kingdom in 721 BCE, a group of persons stayed behind. These persons intermarried with the Assyrians and developed their own religious system. Likewise, the Samaritans usually despised the Jews.

- Why did Jesus use the Samaritan as the hero in the story?

- Who is difficult to show God's love to in your life? Why?

The Good Samaritan not only offers extravagant care by bandaging the wounded man's wounds and taking him to a safe place to heal, but he also promises to return to pay any additional money needed.

- Which is easier for you: to serve others by providing money or direct one-on-one care?

- What do you think happened when the Samaritan returned?

- What is the difference between serving another and befriending another?

- How does befriending another lead us to be an advocate to ensure that the person experiences not only love and compassion but also justice?

- What role did the innkeeper play in the story?

In the story of Mary and Martha, ask yourself whether you are more like Mary or Martha. Share who you most identify with and why.

- What steals your attention from growing closer in your relationship with Jesus?

- How do you balance between sitting at the feet of Jesus and serving others?

General Rule of Discipleship

As we grow deeper in our love of God with our entire heart, being, strength, and mind, we respond by loving others. The United Methodist mission is to witness to Jesus Christ in the world and to follow his teachings through acts of compassion, justice, worship, and devotion under the guidance of the Holy Spirit[17] so that we "make disciples for the transformation of the world."

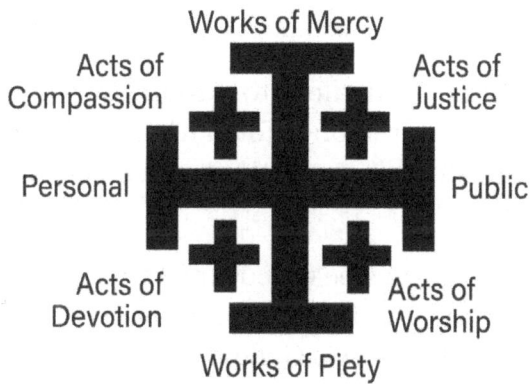

John Wesley's General Rule for Discipleship, which is essential for all Christians, includes personal acts of devotion, acts of compassion, public or communal acts of

---

[17] "The General Rule of Discipleship," *The Book of Discipline of the United Methodist Church* (The United Methodist Publishing House, 2016).

worship, and acts of justice. You may also notice that the acts of devotion and acts of worship lead us to loving God, and the acts of compassion and acts of justice lead us to loving others. Discipleship is both an inward journey and an outward expression of our love. Discipleship is growing deeper in our love of God and our love of others under the guidance of the Holy Spirit.

John Wesley's class meeting system was a three-pronged approach for persons to grow as disciples of Jesus Christ.

1. **Societies,** equivalent to our modern-day worship services, provide a time for the faith community to gather for praise, proclamation of the Word, offering collection for the needs of their communities and across the globe, and a commitment to live as faithful disciples in the world.

2. **Class Meetings,** equivalent to Sunday School and small groups, centered on information into God's Word and faith-forming practices as a disciple of Jesus Christ.

3. **Bands,** equivalent to weekly covenant discipleship groups, are formed around a group covenant where members live out Wesley's General Rule of Discipleship in acts of compassion, devotion, justice, and worship. The group encourages and holds one another accountable in love as persons grow deeper in their discipleship of loving God and others.

Our life as a Christian is usually based on attending worship, being part of a Sunday School class or small group, and actively participating in service or volunteering to serve others in our communities; however, God calls us to a deeper transformation for ourselves and others. In fact, our United Methodist understanding of sanctifying grace is a lifelong journey of always growing deeper in our love of God and service to one another.

Reflection Questions

What do you do each week to grow in your discipleship through:

- Acts of devotion (Bible reading, Bible study, contemplation, prayer, etc.)?

- Acts of worship (attendance, response to worship experience, fasting, generosity, etc.)?

- Acts of compassion for yourself or serving your family, church, and community?

- Acts of justice that befriend another, advocate for another, or respond to an unjust concern in your community?

What area(s) needs more intentionality in your life?

Do you feel you balance your time and resources to loving God and to serving others? Why or why not?

What expectation is there to grow as a disciple of Jesus Christ in your small group? In your church?

Who holds you accountable to grow as a disciple? How?

Next Step

Reflect on today's discussions and reflections. In the space below, write at least one way—but no more than two ways—you will focus on growing as a disciple this next week. Check in on your response at the end of the week and look for successes and areas that could use improvement.

As closing prayer, read the hymn, "Will You Come and Follow Me?"

Lesson 9

The Bible Teaches Us about the Bible
(And Faith in Life and Life in Faith)

Lesson by James Bailes

About the lesson writer:

Dr. Jim Bailes is a retired United Methodist pastor who sought to integrate teaching fully in congregational ministry. He authored and taught Bible studies on local, district, and annual conference levels and in a state prison. He authored the Holston Conference study, Turning Hearts Toward Children.

Scripture Lesson:
Matthew 23:23-26

> *"Woe to you, teachers of the law and Pharisees, you hypocrites! You give a tenth of your spices—mint, dill and cumin. But you have neglected the more important matters of the law—justice, mercy and faithfulness. You should have practiced the latter, without neglecting the former. You blind guides! You strain out a gnat but swallow a camel.*

> *"Woe to you, teachers of the law and Pharisees, you hypocrites! You clean the outside of the cup and dish, but inside they are full of greed and self-indulgence. Blind Pharisee! First clean the inside of the cup and dish, and then the outside also will be clean."*

> **Matthew 23:23-26 (NIV)**

What Do You Think?

Though only twenty-seven, Dietrich Bonhoeffer, by 1936, was already a noted Lutheran pastor, theologian, and teacher throughout Europe. He noticed a profound spiritual malaise with unfortunate spiritual consequences. This spiritual malaise was about to change. Writing a friend in early 1936, he said:

> I plunged into work in a very unchristian way. An ... ambition that many noticed in me made my life difficult. Then something happened, something that has changed and transformed my life to the present day. For the first time I experienced the Bible ... I had often preached, I had seen a great deal of the Church, and talked and preached about it—but I had not yet become a Christian.[18]

In his own words, "something happened" with Dietrich Bonhoeffer. The Bible happened! Bonhoeffer experienced not only the Bible's content but seemingly the Bible's spirit, the living God in and through the Bible. Such spiritual encounters with the Bible resound throughout Christian history—and perhaps in our lives, too. Indeed, the writer of John states his purpose in writing as nothing less than "These things are written so that you may come to believe that Jesus is the Messiah, the Son of God, and that through believing you may have life in his name" (John 20:31).

The Bible proclaims God, working in history through the people of Israel and especially through Jesus Christ. The Bible also teaches us about the Bible, providing hints

---

[18] Eberhard Bethge, Dietrich Bonhoeffer: A Biography (Fortress Press, 2000).

as to how the Bible is to be interpreted and glimpses into what the Bible is and is not. In doing so, the Bible can reveal to us important things about faith in life and life in faith.

What do you think?

Let us study two of the Bible's central proclamations: Creation and Easter morning.

The Bible's Creation Stories

The Bible begins with the resounding affirmation, "In the beginning God created the heavens and the earth" (Genesis 1:1). The Bible's first affirmation is God as Creator, that all there is results from the purposeful actions of God.

We quickly realize (or should) that there are two creation stories! The first is the epic six days of creation and the seventh day of rest (Genesis 1:1-2:4). This majestic creation story begins with "a formless void" (in Hebrew, *tohu-u-bohu*) and darkness. What follows is a poetic, day-by-day, creation part by creation part, with similar beginnings, "Then God said"; similar creative orations, "Let there be"; similar descriptions of God's word becoming tangible creation, "and there was"; and God's evaluation of it all, "and it was good." Very importantly, this first creation story affirms that God blessed God's creation, the animals in Genesis 1:22 and humankind (Adam, "male and female") in Genesis 1:28. (Matthew Fox calls this Original Blessing, explaining that the Bible's

111

"original" story is not sin but blessing). God's blessing continues on the seventh day as God rests, blesses, and "hallows" it (Genesis 2:3).

The first creation story is so well-known and so very revealing, relevant, and telling.

Then we might be surprised to read, "In the day that the Lord God made the earth and the heavens, when no plant of the field was yet in the earth, and no herb of the field had yet sprung up ..." (Genesis 2:4-5). While the first creation story begins and ends with clarity, Genesis 2 returns us to square one—actually before square one. A second creation story immediately follows the first creation story. In contrast to the majestic, poetic structure of Genesis 1, the second story truly is a story. Scholars envision this story being told around a campfire or in the home.

The second creation story tells us that God forms "man" (actually pre-man) from "the dust of the ground" (Genesis 2:7). Man *(adam)* is formed from the ground *(adamah).* But not yet. God then breathes into the earthen figure God's breath (the Hebrew ruach means breath as well as spirit and wind). It is then that the earthen figure becomes Adam, the human being. God's breath has become Adam's breath. Yet God quickly realizes this fellow needs some help, that solitude is not conducive for life, and the woman is created as Adam's helper and partner (Genesis 2:18). (A ludicrous question for the ages: if God had first created the woman, would she have needed any help, a partner?). The story then, and only then, tells us about the remainder of creation.

What we read in the first two Bible chapters is that there are two creation stories proclaiming different orders of creation. Two creation stories yet one spiritual message: God is Creator! The universe, the earth, its creatures, human beings, and all of life are created, created by God.

What do you think? What might this opening Bible affirmation tell us about the Bible more generally with regard to living our faith in particular?

The Bible's Easter Morning Stories

Perhaps the most helpful commentary on the New Testament Gospels is *Gospel Parallels.* This book (in various forms over the years) lists New Testament Gospel passages in parallel columns. Most versions parallel Matthew, Mark, and Luke (called the Synoptic Gospels because they can be literally seen *(optic)* together *(syn)* and are obviously related.) There are versions adding John. This study focuses on Matthew, Mark, and Luke.

A church experience might help us to see these stories better together. For eight years, a church I served presented a powerful Holy Week experience called "His Last Week," four separate presentations of Palm Sunday, Holy Thursday, Good Friday, and Easter. My wife was the dramatic director. "Casting"—searching for a better word—for the first three days was straightforward but not easy. What "characters" would be needed for the empty tomb scene? That's easy! Just read Matthew 28,

Mark 16, Luke 24, and John 20. More specifically, what biblical persons would be portrayed as first going to the tomb and then meeting the visitors there? Simple. Straightforward. Or maybe not.

Who first went to the tomb on Easter morning?

- Matthew 28:1 – "Now after the sabbath, toward the dawn of the first day of the week, **Mary Magdalene** and the other **Mary** went to the sepulcher."

- Mark 16:1 – "And when the sabbath was past, **Mary Magdalene**, and **Mary the mother of James, and Salome,** brought spices so that they might go and anoint him."

- Luke 24:1, 10 – "But on the first day of the week, at early dawn, they went to the tomb, taking the spices which they had prepared" … "Now it was **Mary Magdalene** and **Joanna** and **Mary** the mother of James and the other women with them who told this to the disciples."

- John 20:1 – "Early on the first day of the week, while it was still dark, **Mary Magdalene** came to the tomb and saw that the stone had been removed from the tomb."

The Bible's answer—make that answers—to our question: No two Gospels agree on who first went to the tomb. They agree on Mary Magdalene and no one else. It was the most historic morning of all time, and there is no agreement on who was there.

Who first met these women at the tomb on Easter morning?

- Matthew 28:3 – "And behold, there was a great earth-quake; for an **angel of the Lord** descended from heaven and came and rolled back the stone, and sat upon it."

- Mark 16:5 – "And entering the tomb, they saw a **young man** sitting on the right side, dressed in a white robe."

- Luke 24:4 – "While they were perplexed about this, behold, **two men** stood by them in dazzling apparel."

- John 20:11-12 – "But Mary stood weeping outside the tomb. As she wept, she bent over to look into the tomb; and she saw **two angels in white,** sitting where the body of Jesus had been lying."

The Bible's answer—answers—is that an angel or a young man or two men or two angels were at the tomb. Once again, no two Gospels agree. As with our first question, there are similarities. The young man (or men) may have been angels. His (or their) appearance is similar, yet it is hard to mistake one for two and two for one. Again, as with our brief study of the creation stories, we have seen not two but now four diverse accounts. No two Gospels agree on who first went to Jesus' tomb and who met them there—not even Matthew, Mark, and Luke, which are so similar to one another. Surely, this says something, means something.

What do you think?

What the Bible Just Might Be Telling Us About the Bible (and more)

First: A complete biblical literalism is not biblical.

There have been, are, and undoubtedly will be various ways of understanding scripture. Different ways have developed over the years, some proving to be sound and helpful; others, not so much. Complete biblical literalism is obviously a popular means of understanding the Bible. W.A. Criswell's *Why I Preach the Bible Is Literally True*[19] was—and is—a classic example. (I bought and read this book in my college days. I want my money back, with interest). Dr. Criswell believed that each Bible story should be interpreted literally, each specific detail and central truth. The world was created in six 24-hour days. A whale literally swallowed Jonah. On and on. Dr. Criswell seemed to rest the Bible's credibility and, indeed, the truth of the Gospel on a complete biblical literalism.

The problem is—and was and forever will be—a complete biblical literalism is not biblical! "For the Bible tells me so." Our God-created brains will not allow us to take completely literally both orders of creation in Genesis 1-2. It does not work. Adam cannot be created both last and first. Similarly, our God-created brains— if used, that is—will not allow us to take completely literally the four diverse accounts of Easter dawn. It does not work. This is the Bible talking, the Bible revealing something important about itself. Surely, some things

---

[19] W.A. Criswell, *Why I Preach the Bible is Literally True,* B&H Pub Group, 1969..

are not to be taken literally. Surely, some things are to be taken seriously but not literally.

What do you think? What might be some faith-in-life and life-in-faith implications?

Second: The Bible allows for and affirms diversity.

Creation and Easter. Absolutely basic, foundational biblical affirmations, yet written in diverse ways. God's people receiving the stories recognized this. Genesis, as written in its complexity, was received by the community of faith and passed on through many hands over the years. The people of faith responsible for the Old Testament obviously not only allowed for but seemingly affirmed diversity. There was to be more than one creation story.

The early church surely realized the Easter morning diversity. What were they to do with it and about it? The early church included it, allowed for it, and, in so doing, seemingly affirmed this diversity. This diversity affirmation coincides with early church diversity in general, as seen in all the nations of the world represented at Pentecost (Acts 2), the inclusion of the Gentiles into the faith and the church, the Apostle Paul's teaching of the church, and the Body of Christ and its diversity (1 Corinthians 12, Romans 12), and so forth.

What do you think? What might be some faith-in-life and life-in-faith implications?

Third: The Bible teaches there is unity in the midst of diversity.

The biblical people seemed to have had trouble with this one over the years—the Old Testament people, people in Jesus' day, in the ministry of the apostles, and through the ages. While there are two creation stories, both stories unite in the faith affirmation that God created the heavens and the earth! Whatever the details, as diverse and interesting as they are, the two creation stories are one in affirming God as creator and affirming creation as the handiwork of God.

Similarly, the New Testament Gospels' Easter morning stories, which are so diverse as to who went to Jesus' tomb and who met them there, are united, absolutely united in that Jesus was risen from the dead! Again, in these foundational biblical stories of creation and Easter, the Bible provides unity in the midst of diversity. This reminds us of the worldwide diversity of the Pentecost event populace becoming united in their shared experience of the Holy Spirit. The Apostle Paul's Body of Christ teaching emphasizes unity amid diversity, one body with diverse parts. In these stories and certainly others, the Bible affirms unity amid diversity.

What do you think? What might be some faith-in-life and life-in-faith implications?

Fourth: The Bible teaches that some things are just more essential, more important than others.

The Bible teaches us that there is something more

essential, more important than agreement on literal facts, more important than everyone agreeing on everything or thinking exactly alike, on diversity, which threatens unity but shouldn't. In so doing, the Bible clearly affirms there are some things simply more essential, more important than others.

To list a couple of many possible examples:

- God's expectations for God's people are stated in the Ten Commandments. Though the Old Testament contains 625 commandments, God's priority, as those of the people in their better days, is always the Ten Commandments. The 625 commandments were not regarded as equal to the Ten Commandments and certainly not practiced as such.

- Jesus seeks to teach and live out his understanding of the law's priority. Jesus and, later, Paul affirm it all comes down to love: love of God, love of neighbor, and love of oneself. Jesus derides the Pharisees in Matthew 23:23 by saying, 'You tithe mint, dill, and cummin, and have neglected the weightier matters of the law: justice, and mercy, and faith." To Jesus, there are "weightier matters"; some things are just more essential, more important than others. We remember most of the Jesus-Pharisees' conflict developing from the latter's misunderstanding of this.

What Do You Think? What might be some faith-in-life and life-in-faith implications?

Final Words

John Wesley advocated and sought to practice what he called "the catholic (or universal) spirit." Wesley put it this way:

> In Essentials (essential to salvation), let there be UNITY.
>
> In Non-Essentials (non-essential to salvation, not to mean unimportant), LET US THINK AND LET THINK.
>
> In All Things, let there be CHARITY.

This just might be the lesson of this lesson. What the Bible tells us about the Bible and about life-in faith and faith-in-life.

What Do You Think?

Lesson 10

There is Yet Hope

Lesson by Walter Cross

About the lesson writer:

Walter Cross answered the call to preach in 1992. He attended Emory University, Candler School of Theology in Atlanta, Georgia, completing Pastoral Course of Study. He serves as a mentor for candidates pursuing ministry in the United Methodist Church. Pastor Cross lives in Knoxville, Tennessee, and is the husband of The Reverend Dr. Angela Hardy Cross.

Scripture Lesson:
Romans 4:18-25

> *Against all hope, Abraham in hope believed and so became the father of many nations, just as it had been said to him, "So shall your offspring be." Without weakening in his faith, he faced the fact that his body was as good as dead— since he was about a hundred years old—and that Sarah's womb was also dead. Yet he did not waver through unbelief regarding the promise of God, but was strengthened in his faith and gave glory to God, being fully persuaded that God had power to do what he had promised. This is why "it was credited to him as righteousness." The words "it was credited to him" were written not for him alone, but also for us, to whom God will credit righteousness—for us who believe in him who raised Jesus our Lord from the dead. He was delivered over to death for our sins and was raised to life for our justification.*
>
> **Romans 4:18-25 (NIV)**

A Lesson About Hope from My Mother

It was a pleasant Saturday in autumn in the middle of the 1950s, and I was just a wee little tike. My assignment in that early morning was to assist my mother in preparing food for the church's annual homecoming meal.

My father had recently deposited a ten-pound bag of sweet potatoes in the kitchen, along with a bushel of green beans. I was assigned to help my mother with the prep work, so I scraped the sweet potatoes, which she later cut up and put in a big pot of water to boil. I really wasn't that much help. My mother could have done the job all by herself, but she was helping to entertain me on a Saturday. She knew how to take a green bean, snap it, and pull that long string off it. I could snap a green bean, but my string would always tear off.

The end result of the basket that went to the church the next day was a layer of aluminum foil on the bottom, covered by a clean kitchen towel. My mother transformed those ten pounds of potatoes into four delicious sweet potato pies. I saw every one of them when they went in the oven and when they came out. She used real butter— not margarine like we usually got. They smelled like vanilla, nutmeg, ginger, and all the delicious ingredients.

Next to the pies were two chickens. Two fryers cut up, plus six extra wings. My mother would fry the chicken to perfection in an old black skillet till those caramelized brown pieces would form on the bottom. She would flip the chicken over so easily, with no flash, no pop. That was layer one: the warm layer.

Next, there was a cool layer. On Sunday morning, she put a layer of ice, then twenty-four deviled eggs. Of course, we couldn't take deviled eggs to church, so we called them angel eggs. On top of the angel eggs was a tray of carrots, sweet pickles, and a relish tray. The relish tray had celery, creamed cheese, and little bitty olives.

Next to that tray was a group of toothpicks with Vienna sausages, stuffed olives, and a cube of cheese. They were all lined up like little soldiers. That was the cool layer. She covered that with aluminum foil and another insulating towel.

I got to look at all that food, and then it all went to the preacher's table right after church that Sunday afternoon. I didn't get to eat with the group at the church. Instead, I sat with the organist in the sanctuary while he practiced. I was only five years old, and I would eat my meals at home.

My hope was—yes, there was hope—that there would be something left over from all that chicken and all those pies and all those green beans, that there would be something left for me. I lived in hope. But as the time passed that Sunday, hope began to wane. The preachers were hungry. They asked for seconds. They asked for thirds. Then, they asked for some to take home.

When I went to take the baskets to the car, there was nothing left in the baskets but those towels and some crumpled aluminum foil. I was sad.

I sat in the back seat of the car, thinking, "I'm going to dine on bologna crackers tonight," which would have been okay if I hadn't seen all the fixings my mother had prepared for the meal. But I had seen all of that food.

- I saw all that chicken.
- I saw all those sweet potato pies.
- I saw the green beans.
- I saw all the fixings my mother had made and those homemade brown-and-serve rolls.

And there I sat with an empty basket. My hope was crushed. I sat silently as we went home.

Mother: Walter, Junior. Are you alright?

Me: Yes, ma'am.

Father: Boy, what's wrong with you?

Me: I'm okay, Dad.

I went into the house and sat at the table, anticipating my bologna crackers. My mother looked at me. She almost smiled, but she kept a stern look. She opened the oven. In the back of the oven was pie number five, three chicken wings, and a corner piece of cornbread. Oh, I was so happy.

She looked at me again and said, You thought you got left out. Always remember, there is something for you at home. There is always something for you at home. Patience helps develop hope.

The Hopeless Situation of the Romans

When I turn in my Bible to Romans, the writer is dealing with a situation plaguing the Christians. There's an influx of culture there. The Greek culture and the Roman culture. There's this new movement called "The Way" and a myriad of doctrines, and sometimes it left the new Christians confused. The Old Testament scholars wanted them to adhere strictly to the law. It turns out that the law was neither a friend to them nor a friend to us.

So, Paul steps in and says, "I need to explain something to you all. You all are in a hopeless situation because you've found out you can't keep the law. You're being terrorized by individuals in the religious community who are forcing the law upon you, and they know that you can't keep it because they can't keep it. Your situation appears to be hopeless."

Paul comes to the rescue in Romans, Chapter 8, the rescue chapter for hopeless Christians. Paul gives a list of items that are difficult to deal with:

> *I consider that our present sufferings are not worth comparing with the glory that will be revealed in us. For the creation waits in eager expectation for the children of God to be revealed. For the creation was subjected to frustration, not by its own choice, but by the will of the one who subjected it, in hope that the creation itself will be liberated from its bondage to decay and brought into the freedom and glory of the children of God.*
>
> *We know that the whole creation has been groaning as in the pains of childbirth right up to the present time. Not only so, but we ourselves, who have the first fruits of the Spirit, groan inwardly as we wait eagerly for our adoption to sonship, the redemption of our bodies.*
>
> **Romans 8:18-23 (NIV)**

There is yet hope

Then, in verse 24, Paul says, "There is yet hope. Hope is not something that you can see."

There are two types of hope in the Bible and two types of hope in our lives today. I may hope to win the lottery one day—I don't know how because I don't play the lottery. Winning the lottery is a hope that is defined by chance.

I hope I get a good grade. I hope *Publishers Clearing House* stops by my home and knocks on the door. I hope I get that new car.

That's not what Paul is talking about.

In the New Testament, the word "hope" means *a certainty*. It means it is already done. It means God has handled the situation for us.

Hymn author Edward Mote said it well in 1834:

> *My hope is built on nothing less*
> *than Jesus' blood and righteousness;*
> *I dare not trust the sweetest frame,*
> *but wholly lean on Jesus' name.*[20]

My salvation is done by the finished work on Calvary. I don't hope to be saved. I am. I don't hope to go to Heaven. I'm on my way. Not because of my goodness. It's because—as Paul says—there is nothing remaining that can separate me from the love of God.

> *On Christ, the solid Rock, I stand:*
> *all other ground is sinking sand;*
> *all other ground is sinking sand.*

---

20 Hymn: My Hope is Built, *United Methodist Hymnal* #368.

Can anything ever separate us from Christ's love? Does it mean he no longer loves us if we have trouble or calamity, or are persecuted, or hungry, or destitute, or in danger, or threatened with death? (As the scriptures say, "For your sake we are killed every day; we are being slaughtered like sheep.") No, despite all these things, overwhelming victory is ours through Christ, who loved us.

> *And I am convinced that nothing can ever separate us from God's love. Neither death nor life, neither angels nor demons, neither our fears for today nor our worries about tomorrow—not even the powers of hell can separate us from God's love. No power in the sky above or in the earth below—indeed, nothing in all creation will ever be able to separate us from the love of God that is revealed in Christ Jesus our Lord.*
>
> **Romans 8:35-39 (NIV)**

Not peril, not destruction, not even the idea that we stand on this moment at the brink of World War III. That won't separate me. Not because of the scourge of this dreaded disease that has been sweeping our world for the last few years. Not the crisis in Israel and Gaza. Not the battle between Ukraine and Russia.

That's not going to separate me from the love of God.

- Racism is not going to separate me.
- Hateful speech is not going to separate me.
- Who's president is not going to separate me.
- Who's not the president is not going to separate me.
- What's happening in my family—what's happening in my heart—will not separate me from the Love of God.

It's a done deal.

Reflection Questions

What situations or events in our nation and world make you sometimes feel hopeless?

Are there times when you've felt separated from God? If so, what were some of the causes of those feelings?

How does it make you feel to hear Paul insist there is nothing that can separate you from the love of God?

Made in USA - Kendallville, IN
84693_9781950899821
03.12.2024 0009